Grammar and language study

KEY STAGE
2
PH

impact

WRITING HOMEWORK

Published by Scholastic Ltd,
Villiers House,
Clarendon Avenue,
Leamington Spa,
Warwickshire CV32 5PR

© 1996 Scholastic Ltd
1 2 3 4 5 6 7 8 9 6 7 8 9 0 1 2 3 4 5

UNIVERSITY OF
NORTH LONDON

Activities by the IMPACT Project at the University of North London, collated and rewritten by Ruth Merttens, Alan Newland and Susie Webb, with additional material by Ellika McAuley and Kerry Carter.

Editor Jane Bishop
Assistant editor Sally Gray
Designer Claire Belcher
Series designer Anna Oliwa
Illustrations Mike Miller and James Alexander
Cover illustration Hardlines, Charlbury, Oxford

Designed using Aldus Pagemaker
Printed in Great Britain by Ebenezer Baylis and Son Ltd, Worcester

British Library Cataloguing-in-Publication Data
A catalogue record for this book is available from the British Library.

ISBN 0-590-53378-9

Thanks to the landlord of The Plough at East Hendred for permission to reproduce their sign and to Reed Consumer Books Ltd for 'The Sound of Silence' from 'Winnie the Pooh' by A. A Milne © 1926, A.A Milne (1926, Methuen).

Crown copyright is reproduced with the permission of the Controller of HMSO.

KEY STAGE
TWO

CONTENTS

impact

WRITING HOMEWORK

KEY STAGE TWO

CONTENTS

impact
WRITING HOMEWORK

impact
INTRODUCTION

IMPACT books are designed to help teachers involve parents in children's learning to write. Through the use of interesting and specially developed writing tasks, parents can encourage and support their child's efforts as they become confident and competent writers.

The shared writing programme is modelled on the same process as the IMPACT shared maths which encompasses a non-traditional approach to homework.

This is outlined in the following diagram:

> The teacher selects a task based on the work she is doing in class. The activity may relate to the children's work in a particular topic, to the type of writing they are engaged in or to their reading.

> The teacher prepares the children for what they have to do at home. This may involve reading a particular story, playing a game or having a discussion with the children about the task.

> The children take home the activity, and share it with someone at home. This may be an older brother/sister, a parent or grandparent or any other friend or relation.

> The parents and children respond to the activity by commenting in an accompanying diary or notebook. * This mechanism provides the teacher with valuable feedback.

> The teacher uses what was done at home as the basis for follow-up work in class. This may involve further writing, drawing, reading or discussion.

The activities in this book have been designed to enable children to develop and expand their writing skills in conversation with those at home. Where possible the activities reflect the context of the home rather than the school, and draw upon experiences and events from out-of-school situations.

Shared activities – or homework with chatter!

Importantly, the activities are designed to be shared. Unlike traditional homework, where the child is expected to 'do it alone' and not to have help, with IMPACT they are encouraged – even required – to find someone to talk to and share the activity with. With each task we say the following should be true:
* something is said;
* something is written;
* something is read.

Sometimes the main point of the IMPACT activity is the discussion – and so we do try to encourage parents to see that the task involves a lot more than just completing a piece of writing. It is very important that teachers go through the task carefully with the children so that they know what to do. Clearly not all the children, or parents, will be able to read the instructions in English and so this preparation is crucial if the children are

to be able to share the activity. The sheet often acts more as a backup or a prompt than a recipe.

Diaries

The shared writing works by involving parents in their children's learning. The IMPACT diaries* are a crucial part of this process. They provide a mechanism by means of which an efficient parent-teacher-dialogue is established. These diaries enable teachers to obtain valuable feedback both about children's performances in relation to specific activities and about the tasks themselves. Parents are able to alert the teacher to any matter of concern or pleasant occurrences, and nothing is left to come as a big surprise or a horrible shock in the end of year report. It is difficult to exaggerate the importance of the IMPACT diaries. The OFSTED inspectors and HMI have highly commended their effectiveness in helping to raise children's achievements and in developing a real partnership with parents. * See the Afterword (page 128) for details of where to obtain these.

Timing

Most schools send the Shared Writing activities fortnightly. Many interleave these activities with the IMPACT maths tasks, thus ensuring that the children have something to share with their parents almost every week. Many schools also use the shared writing tasks to enhance their shared reading or PACT programme. It has been found that some parents may be encouraged to take a renewed interest in reading a book with their child on a regular basis when the shared writing project is launched in a class. However, there are a variety of practices and the important point is that each teacher should feel comfortable with how often IMPACT is sent in her class.

Parent friendly

It is important for the success of the IMPACT Shared Writing that parents are aware of both the purpose and the extent of each activity. Many teachers adopt a developmental approach to writing, encouraging emergent writing or the use of invented spellings. Care has to be taken to share the philosophy behind this approach with parents, and to select activities which will not assume that parents are as familiar with the implications as teachers. You will get lots of support if parents can see that what they are doing is helping their child to become cheerful and successful writers!

To facilitate this process, each activity contains a note to parents which helps to make it clear what the purpose of the activity is, and how they can best help. The activities also contain hints to help parents share the activity in an enjoyable and effective manner. Sometimes the hints contain ideas, or starting points. On other occasions they may be examples or demonstrations of how to set about the task concerned.

It is always important to bear in mind that parents can, and sometimes should, do things differently at home. At home, many children will enjoy, and even benefit from, copying underneath a line of text or writing without paying attention to spelling or punctuation, where in school such things might not be expected or encouraged. The most successful partnerships between home and school recognise both the differences and the similarities in each other's endeavours.

Planning

The shared writing activities are divided into four sections according to age: Year 3, Year 4, Year 5 and Year 6. There are two pages of teachers' notes relating to the individual activities at the beginning of each section. When selecting which activity to send home with the children it is helpful to remember the following:

• Ideally, we send the same activity with each child in the class or year. The activities are mostly designed to be as open-ended as possible, to allow for a wide variety of different levels of response. Teachers often add a few extra comments of their own to a particular sheet to fit it to the needs of a particular child or group of children with special educational needs. It is also important to stress that the child does not have to do all the actual writing – often the parent does half or more. The point of the activity may lie in the discussion and the creation of a joint product.

• It is useful to send a variety of different activities. Some children will particularly enjoy a word game, while others will prefer a task which includes drawing a picture. Activities may be used to launch a topic, to support a particular project, to enable a good quality of follow-up to an idea and to revise or practise particular skills. Much of the benefit of the shared writing exercise may be derived from the follow-up work back in the classroom. Therefore, it is very important to select activities which will feed into the type of work being focused upon at that time. For example, if the class is working on grammatical categories, verbs, nouns, etc., then an activity requiring that children and parents produce real and fictional definitions of long words will fit in well. On the other hand, if the class is doing some work on fairy stories, making a **wanted** poster of a character in a story may be appropriate.

Notes to teachers

These give suggestions to the teachers. They outline what may be done before the activity is sent to ensure that it goes

well at home. And they describe how the activity may be followed up as part of routine classwork during the subsequent week. More help with what happens when the activity comes back is to be found in the Afterword on page 128.

Parent letter and booklet

It is very important that parents are kept informed about the nature of this new-style homework. Most schools elect to launch IMPACT Shared Writing by having a meeting or a series of meetings. We have included here a draft letter to parents and a booklet which schools may photocopy and give to parents. The booklet is eight A5 pages when copied, folded and collated. This can be given to all new parents as their children start school. There is a space on the cover for the school name.

Keeping shared writing going...

There are a few tips which have been found over the years to make life simpler for parents, teachers and children:

• Don't send shared writing activities in the first few weeks of the September term. Shared writing, like IMPACT maths, usually starts in the third week of the new school year.

• Don't send shared writing activities in the second half of the summer term. Shared writing, like IMPACT maths, usually belongs to the heart of the school year.

• Do value the work that the children and their parents do at home. Sometimes it may not be presented as you expect – for example, a lot of parents with young children write in upper case rather than lower case letters or will ask children to **write over** a line of print. Remember that what comes back into class is a starting point for work that you consider appropriate, and is facilitating both discussion and partnership.

Dear Parents,

In our class, we have decided to use a new 'shared homework scheme' designed to help develop and improve children's writing skills. This will involve sending home a regular task in the form of an A4 sheet. The sheet will outline a simple writing activity for you and your child to enjoy together. These are designed to be shared; the children are not expected to complete the tasks alone.

We would very much like to talk to you about this scheme, and so on _____ we shall hold three short meetings. You need only come to **one** of these and can choose the time which is most convenient:

• 9.00 in the morning
• 3.30 in the afternoon
• 7.00 in the evening.

We would really like as many parents as possible to attend.

Your help in supporting your child's learning is a crucial part of his/her success at school. We do appreciate the time and trouble that parents take with their children, and we can certainly see the benefits in the quality of the children's work and the enthusiasm with which they attack it.

Please return the slip at the bottom of the letter.

Yours sincerely,

_____

Name _____ Class _____

I would like to attend the meeting at:

9.00 in the morning

3.30 in the afternoon

7.00 in the evening

Please tick **one** time only.

Don't forget...

Pick your time!
When you both want to do the activity.

Don't over-correct!
This can be very discouraging.

Your child does not always have to do all the writing!
You may take turns, or take over sometimes.

Make it fun!
If either of you gets tired or bored help a bit more. Tasks should not last more than 20 minutes unless you want them to!

Praise and encourage as much as you can!

IMPACT

Shared Writing

SPIKe

School name

About Shared Writing

The teacher explains the activity to the class.

The teacher selects an activity

Child and helper read through the activity.

Child and helper talk about the activity.

Child and helper share the writing.

Child and helper comment on the activity in the diary.

Child brings the activity back into school.

Teacher reads the comments in the diary.

The teacher follows up the activity in class.

Spelling and punctuation

We all agree that correct spelling and punctuation are very important. However........

DO

• Notice punctuation when sharing the writing activity.
• Talk about different uses of capital and lower case letters.
• Play word games such as 'I spy' or 'Hangman'.
• Read what the child has written before you make any comment about spelling, punctuation or presentation.
• Help them learn any words sent home by the school.

DON'T

• Worry about every mistake – children can become very anxious about their writing if constantly interrupted.
• With young children don't insist that they spell every word correctly. At this stage we are encouraging them to 'be writers'.
• Don't worry if your child is quite slow to learn to spell and punctuate – these things come with time and encouragement.

How we write

Writing also has a mechanical side, children have to learn to form their letters, to separate words, to begin and end sentences.

When children are first learning to write it can be very discouraging to be constantly corrected. However, as they become more confident, we can afford to draw their attention to certain things.

Becoming independent...

As they get older, children need encouragement to become independent readers and writers. But this doesn't mean that there is no role for a supportive parent. In some ways your help is more and not less necessary...

• Talk about the book they are reading – or even comics or magazines etc. This really helps to encourage children to read.
Ask questions like:
What do you like about this book?
What exciting things happen? Tell me the story...
Which books are good and which are boring?

• Try to read some of the books your child reads. This really gives you a shared experience – and lots to talk about!

• Help them to become confident and independent spellers...

Don't shout because they spell something wrongly!
Do encourage them by looking for letter patterns.
Don't mock a child who finds spelling hard.
Do make a SHORT list of common words and pin it up in the bathroom where everyone sees it every day!

Being a writer...

Is about...
Having ideas
Composing them
Communicating them

Parents can help by...

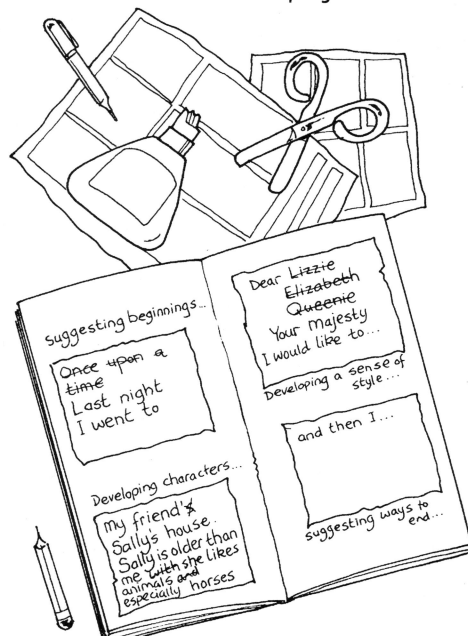

Teachers' Notes
YEAR THREE

Alphabet sentences Make an alphabet book containing a sentence beginning with each letter of the alphabet in turn, and illustrate it. Point out the use of capital letters for beginning sentences. Extend the activity to four letters and focus on including the use of adverbs.

Sentence-swapping Demonstrate this before sending the activity home and play it again back in class. Group the children in a circle and let each child take turns to substitute one element each time. Look at the various parts of speech in each element (verbs, nouns, adjectives).

Sentence chain-gang Ask the children to work in pairs to make concertina books (each page made up of postcard sized card, taped along the left-hand edge to the previous page as they write it). Each pair can write the same sentence on the first page and illustrate it and then make as many sentence chains as possible. Try and make it circular so that the last sentence is the same as the first.

What's my description? Demonstrate this before sending it home. Put the children in pairs, divide them by an eye height screen, give them some pre-drawn pictures on cards and ask them to describe their

pictures to each other, one describing and one drawing. Play a similar game with a 'Treasure Chest' theme. Ask the children to write the directions to find treasure or avoid hazards. Make 'treasure' maps and age them by screwing them up, staining them with tea and warming them in an oven. They make a fantastic display.

Look...no words! Display the range of signs and symbols that the children bring back and discuss the pros and cons of using these rather than written language in certain contexts. Encourage the children to design non-verbal signs for the classroom, school or home such as one symbolising 'no grown-ups' or 'tidy-free-zone' for their bedroom door.

Questions? Questions? Questions? Discuss the children's questions, especially those which don't begin with one of the listed words. Explain how you can reverse the subject and the verb. Use 'hot-seat' role-play to explore the possible answers to the questions about the past or future (which could be linked to your topic work).

Crazy proverbs Discuss real proverbs and their meanings. Give each child a different proverb and set them the task of illustrating it. Divide the class in two and ask one child to hold up their picture to their team who have to try and guess it. If they can't guess it, the opposing team scores a bonus point. Make displays or books of the real and crazy proverb drawings with the written proverbs under flaps.

Too many cooks! Devise some role-play or drama activities to illustrate the proverbs and perform them in class or assembly. Make a display or book collection with explanations. Use them as a source of short story ideas. Have a 'Proverb-story of the week' competition.

Adverb charades Adverb charades is a great game for the classroom especially if you can differentiate it with more difficult examples and with groups of children. Make lists of adverbs as word banks and display them to aid children's writing. Look at the similarities and differences in the spellings of verbs and their adverbs for example, silly and sillily.

Wordy animals Make a book of all the different metaphorical phrases with their pictures. Discuss the characteristics of animal behaviour that have led to the use of such phrases. Look at books that use animal metaphors such as *Mr Gumpy's Outing* by John Burningham (Picture Puffin).

Person-place-thing-ring Play this game in class as a team game with a large board and each child taking turns. Link it to your topic work, for example, 'People, Places and Things' from the Tudors, Romans, Our Locality and so on. Alternatively, give each

group a bank of words on cards and set them the task of sorting them in to categories as a timed game.

Disappearing nouns Ask the children to sort the nouns which they bring in into singular and plural. Remove 'The' and 'plug-hole' from the sentence and set them the task of thinking of more ideas. Sort the words in to groups of common and proper nouns. Use the sentence the child has illustrated for the start of a story.

Where is it? Collect all the prepositions the children have thought of and make a large classroom word bank or book. Make some 'Where's my PE kit?' books in the flap-up style of Eric Hill's *Where's Spot?* (Picture Puffin) books.

Preposition picture Ask the children to design a 'Preposition character' on card and write the preposition on them. Using Blu-Tack, ask the children to fix them to various places on a large picture or frieze. Use it as an interactive display to write some sentences, for example: 'The cow is over the moon' or 'The dog is behind the tree'.

Burst the bubble! Invite the children to read out the comic strips to each other using different voices for each character. Show them how to put speech marks around what was in each speech bubble. Give them strategies for remembering how to do this, 'Speech bubbles burst and the splashes go at the beginning and end of the words spoken'.

Where did it go? Discuss the prepositions the children have listed. Make a preposition flap book, using card to create flaps to look under/behind. Compose a class story entitled 'The Pirate's Treasure' and investigate where the pirate might have hidden the loot? Find out what other weird and wonderful objects are waiting under, behind, over... while your characters search for the lost treasure.

What's he like? See if the rest of the class can discover what the characters' names might be from the children's descriptions. Display the pictures and descriptions in the writing area or in a 'character descriptions' book. Use the descriptions as the basis for creative story writing, allowing the children to choose two or three of the characters for their stories.

Plurals Make two tables one for plurals which 'add an s', and one for 'change the word' words. Make mobiles with the singular form of a word on one side and the plural on the other. Ask the children to choose a word and its plural, for example mouse and mice. Give the children two small paper dessert plates (alternatively use circles or any other shape you wish). They can write the singular word on the bottom of one plate and the plural on the other, and illustrate both. Decorate the scallops that form the edge of the plates. Use wool to stitch the plates together to form a 'flying saucer' shaped disc. Hang these in groups or individually around the room.

Make it negative Ask the children to each read out one of their sentences and then ask another child to make it negative. Then ask the children to read out some negative sentences and ask others to make them positive. Display them on a washing line with a cartoon illustration. Use these statements as the introduction to a story or a newspaper article.

Onomatopoeia Discuss the different onomatopoeia words and look for the most common and most unique. Ask the children to illustrate the words on A5 paper for display or a concertina book, with a different sound effect on each page. In pairs write adventure stories, perhaps in comic form. Incorporate as many different sound effects as possible.

Describe it Display the items and ask the children to read out their descriptions. Display the descriptions near to the items. Ask the class (or a group) to sit in a circle and pass

around various objects. Ask the children to look carefully and each use different words to describe the objects. Add these class descriptions and items to your display.

Quizzy questions Make a wall display or frieze of the questions the children bring back to school. Redecorate the 'question marks' on card or coloured paper and make flap-style question and answers. Make a book using the same format in the shape of a question mark.

Glossy glossaries Make a class book and build up a selection of dictionaries on themes such as sports and hobbies. Use some of the words the children think of for spelling practice. Discuss glossaries in relation to the non-fiction topic books you have in class.

Anno Domini Make some 'Latin root books' around themes such as prefixes and suffixes. Make a frieze or display of objects with word labels in English, Latin and other European languages (such as French, Italian, Spanish, Portuguese) which are heavily influenced by Latin and compare similarities and differences. Make a display of the words in a stained-glass window effect or with illuminated letters.

Scandinavian English Make illustrated word books with the children's word suggestions. Make 'Word-Slides': Cut out two pieces of card to the same size. In one of the pieces, cut out a 'window', this will be the top piece. Attach the two pieces at the side to make a 'wallet'. Next to the window write the letters sk or sc. Make an insert by cutting a strip of paper with suitable word-endings written onto it. Make

sure that you can slide the strip up and down inside the 'wallet' to make different words visible through the window.

Many Englishes Read the poetry of writers who write in dialects and varieties of English, such as John Agard. Can the children imitate the accents of their favourite soap stars?

Get wired! Diagrams are a rich source of writing especially in technology, science and maths. Labelling pictures offers reluctant and developing writers a chance to combine two media. Make a book of electrical appliance circuits sorted in to mains and battery. This could link well with work involving making circuits of various kinds with switches.

Pangrams Compare the children's ideas. Who has the fewest letter duplications? Teach the children other word games and puzzles like word-search, acrostics, anagrams, tongue-twisters, crosswords, word-squares, rebuses and palindromes.

impact WRITING HOMEWORK

Alphabet sentences

Each word in these sentences begins with the next letter in the alphabet.

Ali bought crisps.
Karen loves mushrooms.

● Can you make some sentences like these? Try it with:

(abc) _____

(klm) _____

(rst) _____

impact WRITING HOMEWORK

_____and

child

_____

helper(s)

_____

did this activity together

Sentence-swapping

A simple sentence is often made up of three parts:

For example, **Jack**   **plays**   **in the park**

who?   what?   where, when or how?

● Play this game with your helper: take it in turns to change one part of the sentence at a time. Can you make ten different sentences?

For example, starting with this sentence:

Jack plays tennis... Mehmet plays tennis... Mehmet **likes** tennis... Mehmet likes **dogs... Joanne** likes dogs... Joanne likes **Neighbours...** and so on!

Sentence chain-gang

Can you write a sentence like this?

Mum likes watching **television**. **Television** watching is very popular with our **family**. **Family** life can be difficult when you have to share your **clothes**. **Clothes** get dirty when you play in the **mud**. **Mud** sticks to your shoes.

Each sentence starts with the last word of the sentence before.

● Have a go with your helper to make up some sentences which fit together like this. Take turns to write a sentence each, starting with the last word of the previous sentence. Can you write a chain of ten sentences (five each)?

● Draw some pictures to go with your sentence chain.

To the helper:

● Let your child start. Make it easier by sometimes putting a noun at the end of your sentence. Think about whether you have a verb (a doing or being word) in your sentence.

● Do the task together rather than as a competition and help with ideas and spellings. Remind them that sentences begin with capital letters and end with full stops.

This activity is a playful way of focusing attention on the nature of sentences. In school we will look more closely at the elements of their construction.

_____and

child

_____

helper(s)

_____

did this activity together

impact WRITING HOMEWORK

_____and

child

_____

helper(s)

_____

did this activity together

What's my description?

● On a piece of paper draw a simple picture of something familiar using geometric lines to make squares, triangles and oblongs only.

Don't let your helper see your picture.

● Now describe it to your helper and ask them to draw the same picture from your description. Compare the two pictures, are they the same? Now take it in turns to have another go.

Look...no words!

All these signs mean something but don't use words to explain themselves.

Have you ever seen them before?
Can you find out what they mean?

● Have a look at home and find some other signs like these. Draw them here and explain what they mean.

To the helper:

● Discuss the signs you find on electrical and domestic appliances such as a washing machine and video.
● Have a look at the care labels on clothes or the freezer directions and cooking symbols on food packets. Discuss what they mean especially those that relate to health and safety.

This activity increases children's awareness of conveying messages that don't depend on writing. In class we will look more closely at using signs and symbols as part of our work on developing range in written language.

_____and

child

_____

helper(s)

_____

did this activity together

To the helper:

● Discuss some ideas for questions to ask about the past or the future.

● Help put these ideas in to the form of a series of questions. Remind them about capital letters at the beginning of their sentence and question marks at the end.

This activity gives children the opportunity to think through how ideas can be formulated in to questions and to use the appropriate punctuation.

_____and

child

_____

helper(s)

_____

did this activity together

Questions? Questions? Questions?

When? What? Why? Where? Which? Who? How?

Questions often start with one of these words.

● Think of some questions which you would like to ask someone from the past or someone from the future. Make up seven questions each beginning with one of these words and write them down on a piece of paper.

● Think of another question to ask which doesn't begin with one of these words. Write it down too.

Crazy proverbs

Do you know any proverbs, like these:

'Many hands make light work';
'A stitch in time saves nine';
'Too many cooks spoil the broth'?

What do they mean?

● Now can you make up some crazy proverbs that make no sense at all?

Such as: 'Many cooks make lights work'

● Draw a picture on a piece of paper to illustrate your crazy proverb and write your crazy proverb on the back.

● See if your friends can guess what your proverb is from the picture.

To the helper:

● Mix up the proverbs which you know to make a new crazy proverb or think of one of your own. Try to capture the rhythm which most proverbs have. Discuss what your new proverb means.
● Help with suggestions for putting details in to the picture.

Proverbs capture the wisdom of everyday life in short poetical phrases. They originated before most people could write and so emerged from our oral culture. In school we will be looking at the differences between oral and written language.

_____and

child

_____

helper(s)

_____

did this activity together

_____and

child

_____

helper(s)

_____

did this activity together

Too many cooks!

'Too many cooks spoil the broth' is a well known proverb.

● Ask your helper to help you write down a proverb which they know. Can you also write down what it means?

● Draw a picture to go with it.

Can you find any proverbs from different countries? These are especially interesting.

impact WRITING HOMEWORK

Adverb charades

An adverb is a word used to describe a verb (a verb is a word which describes being or doing). For example, noisily, quietly, quickly, slowly are all adverbs.

● Here's a game to play with your helper.

You think of an adverb, for example 'frantically', but don't tell your helper. Your helper then thinks of an action for you to act out, for example 'brushing your teeth' and you must do this action 'frantically'. Your helper has to guess the adverb.

Take it in turns. Can you guess your helper's adverb?

To the helper:

● Write a list of adverbs and actions you might use in the game as a warm up activity.
● Take turns and think of some more unusual adverbs and actions if the game becomes too easy.
● Write down your new adverbs.

Looking at adverbs is part of our scheme of work on language study which helps children understand the way the grammar of the English language works.

_____and

child

_____

helper(s)

_____

did this activity together

To the helper:

● Make a list of as many animals as you can, and next to each one write down a description of the way the animal behaves for example: 'dog – barking mad'. Help your child with spellings.

● Make suggestions about adding detail to their picture which will capture the meaning of the words or phrases.

This activity looks at the way we use metaphors, in this case about animals, to make meanings in our everyday language.

_____and

child

_____

helper(s)

_____

did this activity together

Wordy animals

Sometimes we use expressions that refer to the behaviour of animals to describe human behaviour. Like this:

'Don't badger me!'

'You're a bully!'

'Stop flapping about!'

Can you think of some more phrases that refer to animals or animal behaviour?

● Write them down.

● Chose one and draw a picture to go with it.

Person-place-thing-ring

A noun is the name of something. It can be of a person, a place or a thing.

● Play this game to see how many nouns you can think of. You will need a coin and a counter each.

● Place your counters on 'Start' and take turns to spin the coin. If you get heads move on two spaces. If you get tails, move one. Depending on the space you land on, you must suggest a noun, of a person, place or thing. Write it in the space with your name to 'claim' that space. Take turns. If you land on someone else's space you miss a go. Play until all the spaces have been claimed. The one with the most spaces claimed is the winner.

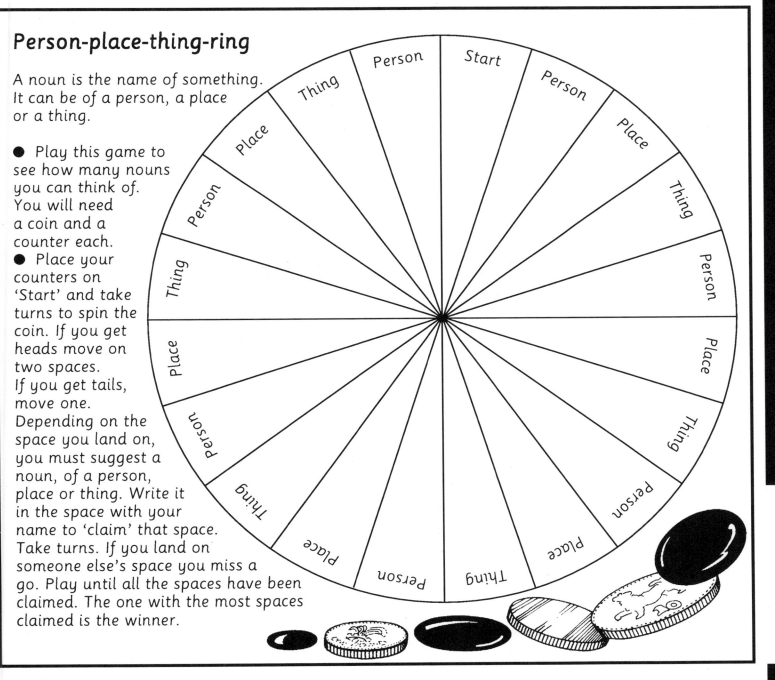

To the helper:

● Think of some people, places and things before you start as a warm-up so the child gets the idea of the differences.
● Help with spellings when writing the nouns in the spaces.
● Give your game a theme so that all the people, places and things have to be 'In our House' or 'At the Supermarket'.

This activity will help the children reinforce work which we are doing in school on nouns and other parts of speech.

_____and

child

_____

helper(s)

_____

did this activity together

_____and

child

_____

helper(s)

_____

did this activity together

Disappearing nouns

Can you fill this gap?

The _____ disappeared down the plug-hole.

How many words can you think of that would fit the blank space and still make sense?

● Make a list on a piece of paper. These words are all the same kind, they are called nouns.

● Choose one of them, write the sentence out and draw a picture to go with it.

Where is it?

When it's time for school do you sometimes lose your PE kit?
Where does your helper suggest you look for it?

● Write down all the places they suggest.

● On a piece of paper, draw a picture of your PE kit in one of the places (but don't make it look obvious!).

To the helper:

● Think of all the places your child leaves things.
● Try to suggest they use 'position' words such as; on, over and beside.
● Help with spellings.

This activity draws the child's attention to prepositions which we will study when looking at the role and functions of different parts of speech.

_____and

child

_____

helper(s)

_____

did this activity together

_____and

child

_____

helper(s)

_____

did this activity together

Preposition picture

A preposition is a word which says where something is.

● Draw your own preposition picture or add to the one below.

● Try to use as many prepositions as you can. Label them.

Burst the bubble!

When you read a comic, the words people say are surrounded by a speech bubble, like this:

In a story, the bubble is burst and the bits of bubble are splashed from one end of the spoken words to the other, like the one below:

The wizard said: 'Abracadabra!'

These are called speech marks.

● Draw a comic strip showing a genie appearing and granting you three wishes. Don't forget to use lots of speech bubbles!

To the helper:

● Talk with your child about what they might wish for. Help them plan their ideas for what to put in each panel of the comic strip.
● Discuss what the spoken words inside the bubbles will be and what the words which tell the story will be.
● Help with spellings, particularly the dialogue.

In class we will express the dialogue using speech marks. This is part of the way in which we study the role and function of punctuation marks in writing.

_____and

child

_____

helper(s)

_____

did this activity together

_____and

child

_____

helper(s)

_____

did this activity together

Where did it go?

● Ask your helper for a 5p coin. Tell them to close their eyes. Now hide the coin somewhere in the room. Explain to your helper how to find the coin. What words will you use to give clues?

● Now let your partner hide the coin and give you instructions on where to find it.

● Take one more turn each and then make a list of all the words you both used to explain where the coin was hidden.

What's he like?

Characters in books are often given names which reflect or describe their personality, their job or a physical trait.

For example:
Mr Sweet may be a kind old man who runs the corner shop.
Rebecca Fidget could be a girl in Year 6 who can't sit still on the carpet and is always wriggling about.

What do you think Nurse Pain would be like? Or Caryna Scarlet?

● Write a short description for each of these characters and read them to your helper. Can they guess the character's name from your description?
You'll have to include plenty of adjectives (words that describe people, places or things) and adverbs (words that describe doing words) in your description.

● On a piece of paper make up a character of your own, write a description and draw a careful picture of your character.

To the helper:

● Does your child's description give a clear and vivid picture of the character? Does the description match the name?
● Help them come up with an interesting name for their own character and a really detailed description.

We have been working on developing characters in our creative writing. The use of adverbs and adjectives in descriptions helps to give well rounded characters and adds interest and meaning to stories.

_____and
child

_____
helper(s)

_____
did this activity together

_____and

child

_____

helper(s)

_____

did this activity together

Plurals

● With your helper, make a list of nouns (people, places and things) on the back of this page.

These words are what one of each thing is called. Do you know what more than one would be called? Sometimes you just need to add an 's' to the end of the word.
Sometimes the word will change completely.

● Try and write the correct plural word next to all your nouns.

Singular	Plural
boy	boys
child	children
mouse	mice

impact WRITING HOMEWORK

Make it negative

● Look at these pairs of sentences. How are the pairs different?

I like chocolate.   **I do not like chocolate.**
There are five boys. **There are no boys.**

The sentences on the right are negative. A negative is a phrase that tells the reader that something is not going to happen, that the writer does not enjoy something or that there are no members in a group.

● Ask your helper to write down five short sentences.

● Rewrite them to make them into negative sentences.

_____and

child

_____

helper(s)

_____

did this activity together

_____and

child

_____

helper(s)

_____

did this activity together

Onomatopoeia

Onomatopoeic words are sound *effect* words.

They sound like the word they describe such as: **sizzle**, **moo**, **woof** and **squeak**.

● Listen to noises around your home and write down the words if you think they are onomatopoeic.

impact WRITING HOMEWORK

Describe it

● Sit in a circle with your helper and some other grown-ups (brothers, sisters, aunties, grandads, anybody). Choose a toy, some clothing, or anything you can see. Set it in the middle of the circle. Tell everyone that you are going to describe the thing. Each person needs to add a new adjective (describing word) to the description. How many different adjectives can you all think of?!

● Ask your helper to write down what you described and all the adjectives you used.

● Bring this list and the item itself into school.

It is a fast, shiny, small, white, toy car

To the helper:

● Help your child select an item that could have many different words to describe it.
● Help them to think of adjectives (describing words) that fit the item.
● Write a careful description of the item using all of your adjectives and please send it into school for part of our display.

We are looking at different parts of speech and their use in writing. We have also been working to make our descriptions more interesting and detailed. Adjectives add depth and meaning to written and spoken work.

_____and

child

_____

helper(s)

_____

did this activity together

_____and

child

_____

helper(s)

_____

did this activity together

Quizzy questions
This is a question mark.

You put question marks at the end of a sentence which is asking a question.

● Think of a question which you are always asking your mum, dad or helper. Write it inside the question mark. Maybe your helper can answer the question by writing it inside or around the dot underneath.

'Can I go to bed late?'
'No!'

impact WRITING HOMEWORK

Glossy glossaries

Offense
Defence
Court
Basket

What do these words have in common?
(and no, they are not about a robber who has stolen an old lady's shopping basket!)
They are all words used in basketball. They have other meanings too of course, but
they have special meanings when used in relation to basketball.

● Do you have a hobby which uses some special words? Write them down with their meanings.

To the helper:

● Discuss with your child which words have special meanings when used in the context of a hobby.
● Show your child how to use a dictionary or show them a glossary in a non-fiction book if you have one.

This activity focuses on how different meanings have become associated with words in different contexts. We shall discuss and explore the way meanings have developed in technical, commercial, industrial and other contexts as part of our schemes of work for language study.

_____and

child

_____

helper(s)

_____

did this activity together

_____and

child

_____

helper(s)

_____

did this activity together

Anno Domini

When the Romans invaded Britain in 43AD they brought with them their language – Latin. When they left Britain nearly 400 years later, most people in Britain had been converted to Christianity. The Church authorities wrote mainly in Latin and so many words we use in English today have their roots in Latin, words like: **angel, bishop, candle, school, hymn, nun, fountain** and so on.

● What other words do you know associated with the Christian faith? Make a list of the words and put an 'L' next to the ones you think might have Latin roots.

impact WRITING HOMEWORK

Scandinavian English

In the 9th Century the Vikings invaded Britain from Scandinavia speaking a language called Old Norse. Many of the words we use today in modern English that begin with **sc** or **sk** come from the Old Norse language, words such as **scale**, **scratch**, **scout** and **sky**, **skirt**, **skip**.

● How many words beginning with **sc** and **sk** can you think of?

● Make two lists.

To the helper:

● Simply 'brainstorm' all the words you can think of together and write them down under two headings.

● If you have a dictionary you could use that to maximum effect!

This activity is intended to arouse interest in the history and roots of the English language. Old Norse is an important source of many of the most commonly used words in English, particularly in the north of England.

_____and

child

_____

helper(s)

_____

did this activity together

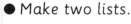 **WRITING HOMEWORK**

_____and

child

_____

helper(s)

_____

did this activity together

Many Englishes

English is used, with a very rich diversity of accents and dialects, around the world in places like the United States of America, Australia, India, the Caribbean, South Africa and elsewhere. But you don't have to go to the other side of the world to hear these accents. Turn on your TV and listen out for them.

● Make a list of as many people as you can from TV, radio, video or films who speak English with one of these accents:

Liverpool 'Scouse'

Australian 'Strine'

Jamaican

London 'Cockney'

American

Newcastle 'Geordie'

Get wired!

● Choose an electrical appliance in your home. Make a drawing of the electrical circuit and label all the parts.

● Make a list all the things in your house that work on **mains** electricity and all the things that work on **battery** power.

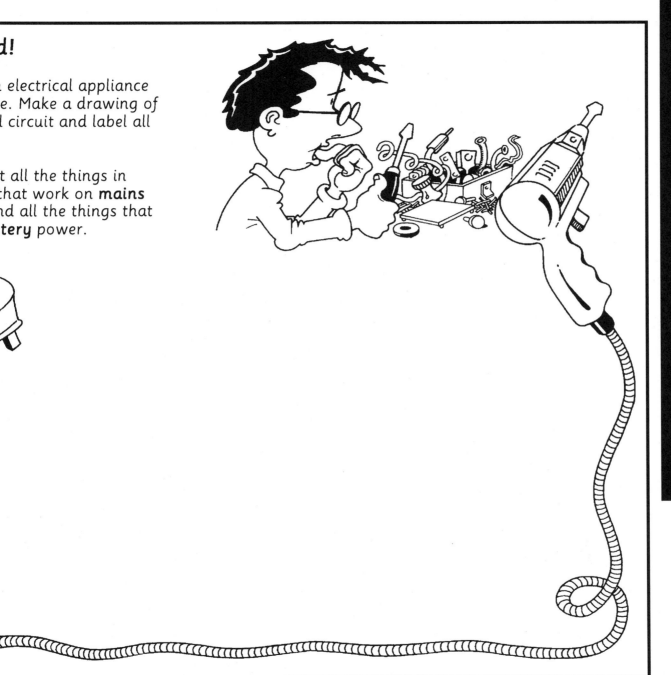

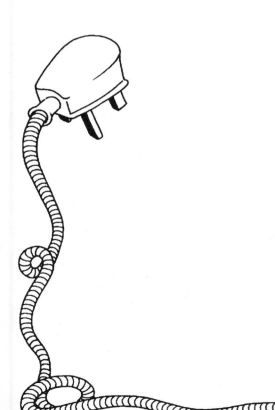

_____and

child

_____

helper(s)

_____

did this activity together

_____and

child

_____

helper(s)

_____

did this activity together

Pangrams

A pangram is a sentence which includes every letter of the alphabet.

The quick brown fox jumps over the lazy dog is a famous pangram.

● Can you write a sentence like this? Don't forget, you must use every letter in the alphabet!

Teachers' Notes
YEAR FOUR

Group it! List the collective nouns and add any that the children may have discovered. They can be illustrated by children working in pairs and displayed in the writing area. Using the original list see how many other nouns the children can produce for each 'group' word. For example pairs of: pants, trousers, scissors, packs of: dogs, wolves, cards. Can the children find any common factors to these, such as pair – two things; pack – lots of things?

Sentence alliteration Before giving the homework, assign letters to the children, perhaps two or three each. When they return ask the children to read their sentences out loud and to illustrate them for a wall display or concertina book so that all the letters of the alphabet are represented.

Weather words Working in pairs or small groups ask children to search for the meanings of the 'weather words'. Display the words and meanings in a mobile or on a weather map. Ask the children to write a weather forecast and draw a map, using correct symbols to match. Ask them to include important places. Record the forecasts and have the tape available with a book showing forecasts and weather maps.

Ups and downs Make a class list of all the prepositions and discuss their meanings. Ask the children to illustrate them and display them as a mobile. Stitch two small paper plates together back–to–back and write a word on either side (for example, 'up' on one side, 'down' on the other). Illustrate the prepositions and decorate the plates. Hang these in groups or individually around the classroom.

Spiral word game Make some copies of this game mounted on card so that children can play it in pairs when they have finished work early. This could also be linked to a class topic to develop the vocabulary or word bank. Make it more difficult by adding new rules such as, 'no proper nouns/all verbs in the past tense'.

Fill that gap! Set the children exercises on the word lists they bring back such as sorting them into present and past tense. Ask the children to convert them from one to the other or to convert them into future tense if possible. Look at verbs that change their vowel sounds in the past tense for example, throws – threw.

Adjective acrostic Ask the children to rewrite and design their acrostics for a wall display. You could use illuminated initial letters and add other graphic designs to elaborate the adjectives. Extend the activity to include surnames or words from the current topic. Make some adjective cubes to describe their character: 'The six sides of me'.

Descriptive details Before they take this activity home show the children a Children's Thesaurus. Make a word bank of adjectives to display in class or make a class Thesaurus.

Choose a character from a class reading book and think of as many adjectives as possible to describe that character. Write an 'Eye Witness' description from a photograph of someone unknown to the children.

Can't, shan't, won't! Before sending this activity home, discuss with the children the use of the apostrophe to symbolise missing letters. Make a list of words which use an apostrophe in this way and the words they have shortened. Back in class, ask the children to read out their excuses. Can they write a short play script, poem or story? (Read *Not Now Bernard* by David McKee (Andersen Press)).

Commander Comma Demonstrate the use of the comma in lists before sending this activity home. Ask the children to read their lists to each other and guess the destination. Illustrate them or make a book with the destination covered by a flap. Use the lists as ideas for creative writing.

What's in a name? Look at other colloquialisms and their origins and meanings. Ask the children to research these in good dictionaries. Look at other examples of how names have entered the language as verbs (such as, hoover). Collect as many as you can and set the children a task of including them in a story, comic strip, poem or sequence.

Invented words Make a display with the drawings and words. See if any are in the dictionary (you may need a good one like OED, Chambers or Websters). Read the

children some funny poems of families, friends and teachers from poets like Hughes, McGough, Patten, Rosen and the Ahlbergs. Help them to write funny poems using their invented words and phrases.

Do you read me? Demonstrate this activity before you send it home. Learning the Phonetic Alphabet could be a source of many activities, games and fun tests in the class such as Phonetic Bingo. Children could devise adventure board games which challenge them to de-code phonetic messages in order to pass on from one point to the next.

The beginnings of writing/Egyptian hieroglyphs Salt dough can be made by mixing equal amounts of flour and salt and then adding water until you have the right consistency. There will be many opportunities for displaying the results of the cuneiform/hieroglyphic slabs. Decorate them, hang them. Put coded messages on them.

Add on Latin/Re-visit ex-citing Latin! Make and display mobiles of the words children bring back, highlighting the focal root word. Have 'Latin Quiz' games where the children have to guess the definition of a word and check it against the dictionary, winning points if they are correct or nearly so. Find other Latin root words to generate lists of words which will be of relevance to topics, themes or issues. Use roots as a strategy for spelling technique.

It's all Greek to me! You can do some mathematical activities with these root words looking at the number of combinations and permutations that can be generated from them. Express them in the form of Venn diagrams. Devise some card games or pelmanism activities where the children have to turn over and pair up combinations. Make a Greek or Latin dictionary or a flip-flap book so that combinations can be generated by turning various pages.

Old English Ask the children to put their lists into alphabetical order or play dictionary games like writing out the lists on cards, dealing them out to groups and setting the children timed tasks of finding the words in dictionaries. Rather than competing against each other, they could time themselves to improve dictionary speed. Make a large painting, collage or frieze of a farm with each child providing a different animal, tool or machine. Label them.

Accent map of Britain Display a large map of the UK and plot the various accents and dialects. Read the poetry of writers who write in dialects and varieties of English. Records and tapes are available from the BBC illustrating varieties of English. Can the children imitate the accents of their favourite soap stars?

Give me a sign Demonstrate the activity before sending it home. Make a Sign Alphabet Book. Ask the children to learn the entire alphabet and encourage them to 'talk' in class using signing! Have class sessions of translating and interpreting. Invite a fluent signer in to demonstrate other aspects of signing. The alphabet reproduced here is used in England, Scotland and Wales. An Irish Standard Manual Alphabet is used in both Northern Ireland and the Republic of Ireland and is quite different to the Standard version. Teachers can write to the RNID for copies of the Irish Standard Alphabet. Write to RNID (NI), Wilton House, 5 College Square North, Belfast BT1 6AR. Explore other sign systems like Braille, see page 96.

Greetings! Compare the diversity of the material the children bring back by encouraging them to each speak a different greeting. Look at the ones that draw on different accents, dialects, languages and cultures (like the seasonal greetings). Compare types: formal and informal; written and spoken; ethnically based; gender based and occupation based.

Mistake and identify Play a 'Spot the difference' game; lay out a tray of small objects, let the children scan the tray, then turn away. Change the objects so some have

been omitted, some added, some substituted, some inverted. Then when they turn back they have to identify which. Ask them to proof-read their own or their partner's writing and try to identify examples from each type.

The Word Make a display of sacred texts and artefacts from various religions. Every religious group uses stories, myths and legends to pass on its values – read a selection to the class. Invite local religious leaders to speak about the texts sacred to their religion and explore other aspects of the writing such as script, language, history or the paper or material it is written on.

Get spaced out! Set the children coding and decoding activities based around changing word spacing. Ask them to read the new phoneme codes to each other to see if they can 'hear' the original. Look at the word spacing conventions on word processors like ragged edge and justified, and of other languages like Bengali, Gujerati, Chinese. See Crystal, D. (1987) *The Cambridge Encyclopaedia of Language* (Cambridge University Press) pp 64-65 for more ideas on this.

A name, not a number! Make a display of the various forms of identity children bring in. Display a map of all the different birthplaces, graphs of birth dates, photos of children identified by their 'numbers'. Discuss and write about how they would feel about living in a society where they were identified by a number rather than their name.

Silent sections Before you send the activity home explain it by using an example of dialogue that will lend itself to a silent

response like David McKee's *Not Now Bernard* (Andersen Press). Display the various ways children have chosen to express silence (they won't be easy to read aloud!). Look at some books to find other ways of showing vocalisation in writing such as bold lettering, italics, sizing letters, capitalisation and letter repetition.

Matrices Look at data handling software on computers using alpha-numeric data. Introduce concepts like field and cell. Devise uses for matrices and databases within your current topic work or for classroom jobs, tasks and record-keeping. Display and compare the finished results.

Super-word! Look at the endings of the words and explore their meanings for example, sonic, natural and so on. Make word-slides (two pieces of attached card, the top piece with a window cut-out. Write the word *super* on the top piece, next to the window. Write the word endings on to a strip of card and slide them up and down in between the two pieces of card to make different words visible through the window. See the diagram on page 12).

Sub–stitute your pre–fix! Make and display mobiles of the words children bring back, highlighting the focal root word. Have 'Latin Quiz' games where the children have to guess the definition of a word and check it against the dictionary, winning points if they are correct or nearly so. Find other Latin root words to generate word lists of relevance to topics, themes or issues. Display them as word banks around the classroom. Use roots as a strategy for spelling technique.

Group it!

A group of fish swimming together is called a school of fish. In the same way a group of steps is called a flight.

● Can you match these group words to the correct items?

● On a piece of paper, write a short sentence for each of the pairs. Such as 'I bought a bunch of grapes at the shop'.

Can you or your helper think of any other group words?

Group word	Items
bunch	socks
chest	cattle
set	people
crowd	drawers
flock	grapes
herd	tools
pack	birds
pair	wolves

To the helper:

● Talk with your child about the group names and help them to use the names in a sentence. Talk about why we need to group things in conversation. Do any of the group words name groups for more than one item (pair – trousers, socks, pants, for example)?

We have been studying parts of speech in our language work. Collective nouns are used to identify groups of a particular item and add depth to writing.

_____and

child

_____

helper(s)

_____

did this activity together

_____and

child

_____

helper(s)

_____

did this activity together

Sentence alliteration

● Write a sentence where as many words as possible begin with the same letter. For example, for the letter 'b' you could write: the big boy bravely bounced the blue ball.

● Try to use adjectives and adverbs in your sentence to make it more interesting.

● Write sentences for these letters:

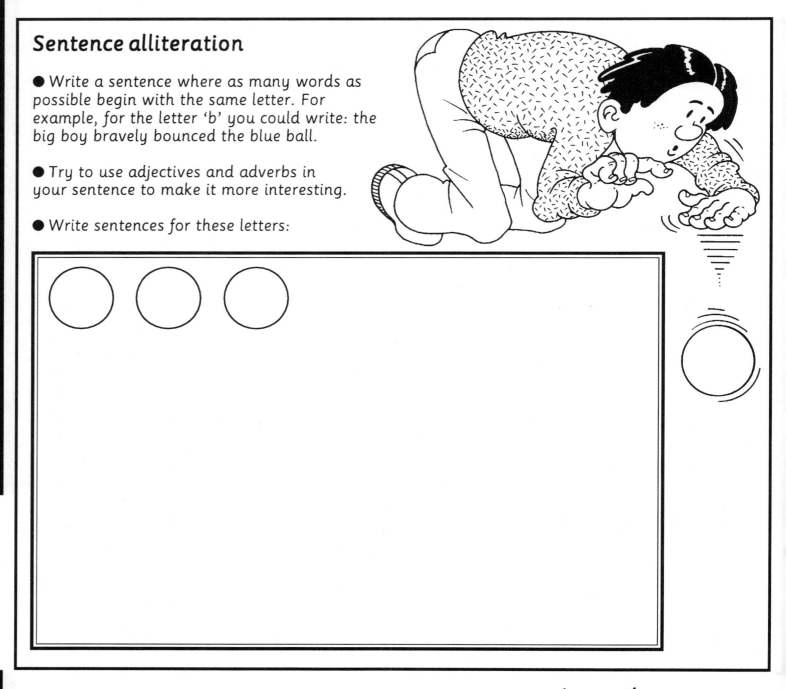

Weather words

Listen to a weather forecast on the radio or television or read one in a newspaper. Do you notice any words which are used in the forecast that are not common in everyday language? Are everyday words used in a different way than how they are usually used?

● Make a list of the words you found.

_____and

child

_____

helper(s)

did this activity together

_____and

child

_____

helper(s)

_____

did this activity together

Ups and downs

When you explain to someone where something is you often use prepositions to give its location. It could be 'Up on the shelf' or 'Down the stairs'.

● Think of as many place words as you can and their opposites. Make lists of them here.

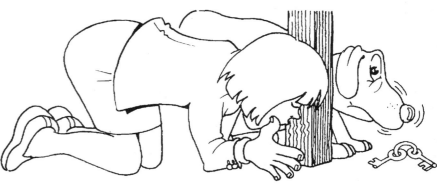

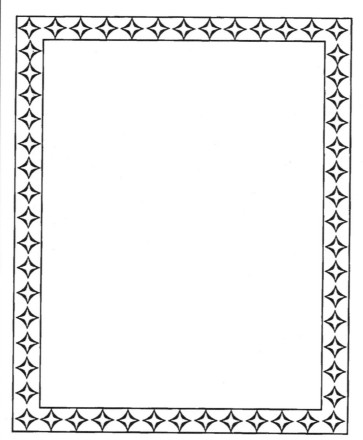

Spiral word game

A noun is a word naming a person, place or thing.

A verb is a word describing being or doing.

Here's a game you can play about nouns and verbs! You will need a coin to spin and a counter for each player.

● Begin with your counters on the 'start'. Take turns to spin a coin. 'Heads' move one space. 'Tails' move two. You must think of a word for the space you land on and write it down. If you can't think of a word or if you get it wrong you must stay where you are. First one to the centre wins. (You must think of a new word each time, you can't repeat one that's already been used!)

Start

Verb · Noun

Verb · Noun

Noun · Verb

Noun · Verb

Noun · Noun · Verb · Verb

Noun · Verb

Noun · Verb

Winner

Verb · Verb · Noun · Noun

Verb · Noun

Verb · Noun

Verb · Noun

Noun · Verb

Noun · Verb

Noun · Verb

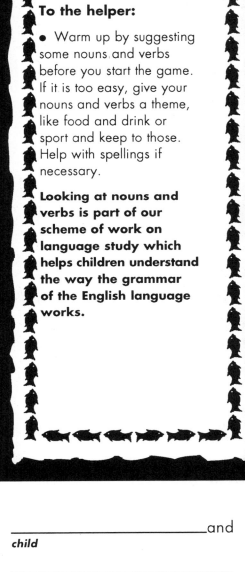

To the helper:

● Warm up by suggesting some nouns and verbs before you start the game. If it is too easy, give your nouns and verbs a theme, like food and drink or sport and keep to those. Help with spellings if necessary.

Looking at nouns and verbs is part of our scheme of work on language study which helps children understand the way the grammar of the English language works.

_____and
child

_____
helper(s)

_____

did this activity together

_____and

child

_____

helper(s)

_____

did this activity together

Fill that gap!

Our cat _____ a mouse.

How many single words can you think of that will fill the gap and still make sense?

● Make a list of them. Choose one of the words to put in the gap and draw a picture to go with it.

impact WRITING HOMEWORK

Adjective acrostic

Adjectives are words which describe people, places and other things.

● Write your name down the side of the page and think of an adjective beginning with each letter of your name, like this:

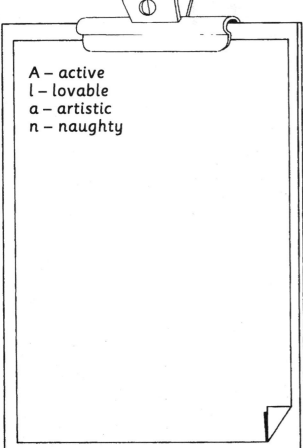

A – active
l – lovable
a – artistic
n – naughty

_____and

child

_____

helper(s)

_____

did this activity together

_____and

child

_____

helper(s)

_____

did this activity together

Descriptive details

My _____ sister ran across the road.

What words could you put in the gap?
These words are likely to be adjectives;
words that describe a person, place or thing.

● Write a list of all the adjectives that will make sense here.

impact WRITING HOMEWORK

Can't, shan't, won't!

What do you say to your mum, dad or helper when you don't want to do something they want you to do?

> I can't do it!

> I won't!

● Write down what else you might say when you are resisting someone!

What does your mum, dad or helper say when they don't want to do something that you want them to do?

> I haven't got time at the moment!

> Ask your sister!

● Write down some more phrases they say when they are resisting!

● Put a ring around all the phrases (or highlight them with a highlighter if you have one) that have an apostrophe which looks like this: '
This is used when a letter or a space is missed out.

To the helper:

● Warm up by thinking of all the times when you make excuses and what you say.

● Focus on the ones which include apostrophes and help your child put the apostrophe in the right place.

● Discuss the letters and spaces that have been missed out and what the words have been shortened from.

This activity helps children understand how and why we use apostrophes in written language to show the contractions of oral speech. We will look more closely at these back at school.

_____and

child

_____

helper(s)

_____

did this activity together

Commander Comma

Commander Comma is planning a holiday. Can you work out where he is going?

● Answer these questions by writing a sentence and putting commas between each answer (apart from the last two where you put an 'and'. Bring your answers back to school. Can your friends guess where he is going?

1. What did he wear?
2. What did he take?
3. Whom did he take?
4. What did he do there?

_____and

child

_____

helper(s)

_____

did this activity together

What's in a name?

Did you know that the flushing toilet was invented by a man named Mr Crapper?
It's true!
Do you know any other machines or inventions named after the people who invented them?

● Make up an inventor's name and a story about the invention to go with it.

For example, how about the fictional Mr Headover Heels, a high class cobbler who invented platform shoes. Unfortunately he made his own ones too wobbly and he tripped over his own feet!

To the helper:

● 'Brainstorm' some ideas and examples. Think of domestic electrical appliances and some industrial machinery to get the ideas flowing. Help with spellings if necessary.

This activity is intended to arouse an interest in the origin and use of colloquial (everyday) phrases and to use them as a starting point for a story.

_____and

child

_____

helper(s)

_____

did this activity together

To the helper:

● Make suggestions for funny invented words or phrases. Start with words that refer to a person's appearance or personality.

● Perhaps you could try to remember some of the words and phrases which you used to describe your teachers when you were at school.

● Help with spellings.

New words are being invented all the time and some become part of accepted language. This activity looks at the way language changes and is constantly re-inventing itself.

_____and

child

_____

helper(s)

_____

did this activity together

Invented words

'Grotty Head' was a phrase invented for the Beatle, Ringo Starr in the film 'A Hard Days Night'. What do you think it means?

● Invent some new words and phrases for the appearance of:
– your friends;
– your teachers;
– your family.
Make them funny and draw some pictures to go with them!

Do you read me?

'This is India, Mike, Papa, Alfa, Charlie, Tango.
Are you reading me? Over.'

The Standard International Phonetic Alphabet was devised to reduce confusion and uncertainty of pronunciation for mariners and pilots using radio communications. Here is the full phonetic alphabet.

A	Alfa
B	Bravo
C	Charlie
D	Delta
E	Echo
F	Foxtrot
G	Golf
H	Hotel
I	India
J	Juliet
K	Kilo
L	Lima
M	Mike
N	November
O	Oscar
P	Papa
Q	Quebec
R	Romeo
S	Sierra
T	Tango
U	Uniform
V	Victor
W	Whiskey
X	X-Ray
Y	Yankee
Z	Zulu

● Write down your name in the Phonetic Alphabet and learn it.

● Write a message using the phonetic alphabet.

To the helper:

● Discuss the various emergency and military services that use the phonetic alphabet and why it is necessary. You can play at testing each other on remembering phonetic messages.

This activity focuses on an interesting and potentially useful aspect of language. Children who take part in outdoor activities such as sailing or go on to be members of scouts, guides or cadet corps will find it especially useful. Learning and using the phonetic alphabet will also help to improve spellings.

_____and

child

_____

helper(s)

_____

did this activity together

_____and

child

_____

helper(s)

_____

did this activity together

The beginnings of writing

Writing is thought to have first been invented to keep records of trade and commerce. The earliest known form of writing was done by the Sumerians (in what is now Iraq) about 5,000 years ago. They pressed a cut reed in to wet clay to leave a wedge shaped mark called a cuneiform. It was known only to very important people. It looked like this:

● Make some salt dough (using equal parts salt and flour and mixed to a paste with water) and roll it out to make a slab. Use a cut drinking straw or lollipop stick to make up your own cuneiform message!

Don't forget what your invented message means!

Egyptian hieroglyphs

The Egyptians invented a writing system called hieroglyphics which means 'sacred carving'. It was a secret system of writing known only to very special people. It looked like this:

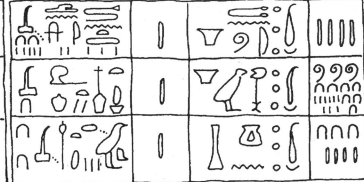

● Make some salt dough (using equal parts salt and flour and mixed to a paste with water) and roll it out to make a slab. Use a cut drinking straw or lollipop stick to make up your own hieroglyphic message!

Don't forget what your invented message means!

To the helper:

● Talk about why hieroglyphics was a secret system known only to important and special people. Use Plasticine if you don't have time to make salt dough.

This activity is intended to arouse interest in the origins and development of writing, but it will be fun to do as well!

_____and

child

_____

helper(s)

_____

did this activity together

_____and

child

_____

helper(s)

_____

did this activity together

Add on Latin

The Romans brought Latin to Britain when they invaded in 43AD. They left us with many words we now add on to words in our everyday speech. These 'add on' words are called prefixes when they come at the beginning of the word. For example: **inter** is a Latin prefix meaning 'between' or 'among'. There are now hundreds of words in English with this Latin prefix such as:

interchange　　　**inter**national　　　**inter**com

● How many words can you think of with **inter** as a prefix? Make a list here.

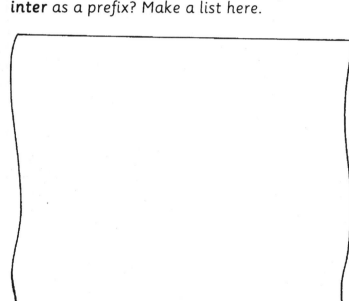

Multi is another prefix meaning 'many' or 'much' from the Latin word 'multus'. There are now **multi**ple examples of words in English with this Latin prefix such as **multi**storey, **multi**millionaire and so on.

● How many can you think of with **multi** as a prefix? Make another list.

impact WRITING HOMEWORK

Re-visit ex-citing Latin!

The Romans brought Latin to Britain when they invaded in 43AD. They left us with many words we now add on to words in our everyday speech. These 'add on' words are called prefixes when they come at the beginning of the word. For example: **re** is a Latin prefix meaning 'again'. The English word repair (**re** + pair) comes from the idea of 'putting a pair together again'. There are now hundreds of words in English with this Latin prefix such as **re**fuse, **re**venge, **re**peat, **re**distribute, **re**house and so on.

● How many words can you think of with **re** as a prefix? Make a list.

ex is another Latin prefix meaning 'out of'. There are now hundreds of words in English with this Latin prefix such as **ex**hibition, **ex**it, **ex**haust, **ex**-directory and so on.

● How many words can you think of with **ex** as a prefix? Make a list.

To the helper:

● You don't need to know any Latin to do this activity! Simply write down all the relevant words you can think of.

● Use a dictionary if you have one or scan the pages of a newspaper or magazine – you will soon come across some examples.

This activity is intended to arouse interest in the origin of words, known as etymology, and help children understand some aspects of English grammar. We will be exploring this more in school as part of our scheme of work on language study and standard English.

_____and

child

_____

helper(s)

_____

did this activity together

_____and

child

_____

helper(s)

_____

did this activity together

It's all Greek to me!

Over the centuries scholars and learned people have used the knowledge passed down by the ancient Greek civilisation. Many of the words from the Greek language are still used, such as:

graph	tele	naut	micro
phone	scope	astro	photo

● How many words can you make using combinations of these Greek root words? Make a list.

impact WRITING HOMEWORK

Old English

For nearly four hundred years (from the 4th century to the 7th century) Angles and Saxons from northern Germany were settling in southern Britain and bringing with them their language known as Old English. They were highly skilled in agriculture and animal farming and many of the common words we use in modern English today come from that time, words like: **crop, field, farm** and **cow, goose, hen** all come from Anglo-Saxon Old English.

● Make a list of as many words as you can think of to do with agriculture, farming and farm animals.

To the helper:

● Start by 'brainstorming' all the words you can think of such as *plough, horse, tractor, barn* and *combine harvester*. Help with spellings.

● Discuss which words you think are old (like *horse*) and which words are comparatively new (like *combine harvester*) and write *OE* for *Old English* or *NE* for *New English* next to each one.

This activity is intended to arouse interest in the origin of words, known as etymology. In school we will be using dictionaries to further explore word origins and meanings.

_____and

child

_____

helper(s)

_____

did this activity together

_____and

child

_____

helper(s)

_____

did this activity together

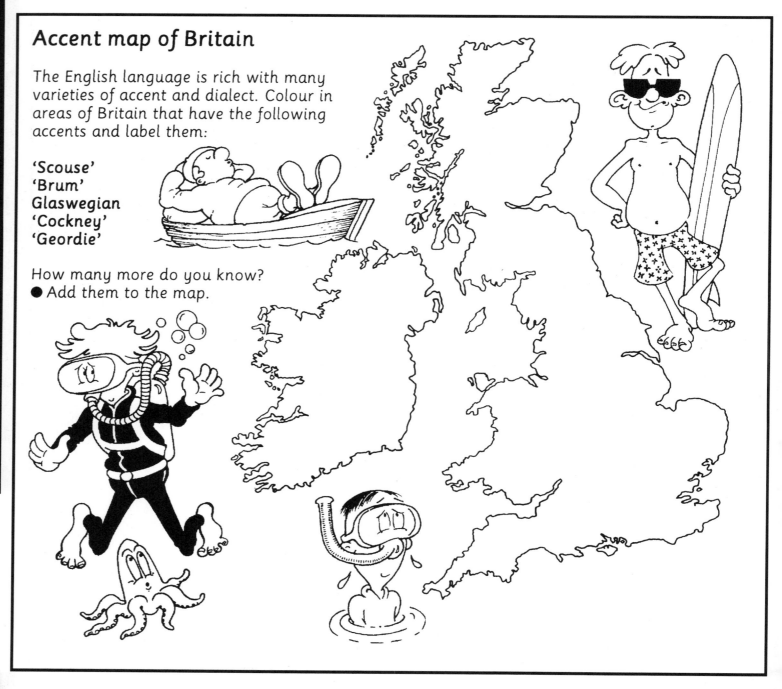

Accent map of Britain

The English language is rich with many varieties of accent and dialect. Colour in areas of Britain that have the following accents and label them:

'Scouse'
'Brum'
Glaswegian
'Cockney'
'Geordie'

How many more do you know?
● Add them to the map.

Give me a sign

Here is the alphabet of the British Sign Language.

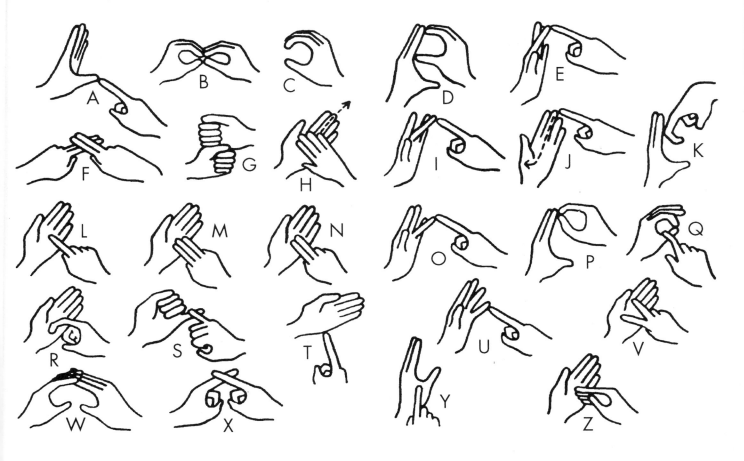

Many people who are hearing-impaired use this finger spelling system.

● Can you learn to spell your name in sign language?

Reproduced with kind permission of the RNID

To the helper:

● It is not difficult to learn this alphabet. Talk about the finger shapes needed for each letter of your name and suggest ways of memorising it.
● If your child finds it easy and fun suggest learning the names of everyone in the family or the whole alphabet, it won't take long!

This activity provides the opportunity for children to learn the alphabet of British Sign Language and explore signs as systems of written language known as dactylology.

_____and

child

_____

helper(s)

_____

did this activity together

_____and

child

_____

helper(s)

_____

did this activity together

Greetings!

● Write down all the different ways that you can say:

a greeting (for example: Hi! How are you doing? Hey up Missus!)
a farewell
an introduction
a toast
an apology
thanks
seasonal or festive greetings
congratulations

Mistake and identify

When we make spelling mistakes they are nearly always one of the following types:

an omission: when we leave out a letter, for example **botle** (for bottle)

an addition: when we add a letter, for example **misstake** (for mistake)

a substitution: when we put a letter in place of another, for example **independance** (for independence)

an inversion: when we have all the letters correct but we swap some around, for example **tabel** (for table)

In this passage from Robert Louis Stevenson's *Child's Garden of Verses* we have added spelling mistakes to the poem 'Windy Nights'. But can you identify how many and which type they are?

● Put a circle around each mistake. Then write out the type headings and put the spelling mistakes next to them. Can you add the correct spellings of the words too?

Whennever the moon and stars are set,

Whennever the wind is high,

All nihgt long in the dark and wet

A man gos riding by.

Late in the nihgt, when the fires are out,

Why does he gallup and gallup about?

Whennever the trees are crying aloud,

And ships are tosed at sea,

By, on the highway, low and loud,

By at the gallup gos he.

By at the gallup he gos, and then

By he comes back at the gallup again.

To the helper:

● Put a circle around the words that don't appear to be spelled correctly. Talk about what type of spelling mistake it is.
● Write out your own attempts and compare them.
● Use a dictionary to check them if you have one.

By helping children identify the types of spelling errors that are common, this activity will help them improve their ability to edit and proof-read written language.

_____and

child

_____

helper(s)

_____

did this activity together

To the helper:

● Talk about any stories or prayers that the children may have been taught at home or at your place of worship. They may find writing some of this particularly difficult if it is in language unfamiliar to them.

● If you have any of these sacred texts at home, get them out and look for a suitable passage the children can write about.

This activity is intended to arouse interest in how writing can be considered sacred and holy. It will form part of the work we will do in school on language study and religious education.

_____and

child

_____

helper(s)

_____

did this activity together

The Word

All major world religions have sacred writings and holy scriptures. Can you match these holy scriptures to their religions?

The Bible	Islam
The Koran	Judaism
The Vedas	Sikhism
The Guru Granth Sahib	Christianity
The Pali Canon	Hinduism
The Torah	Buddhism

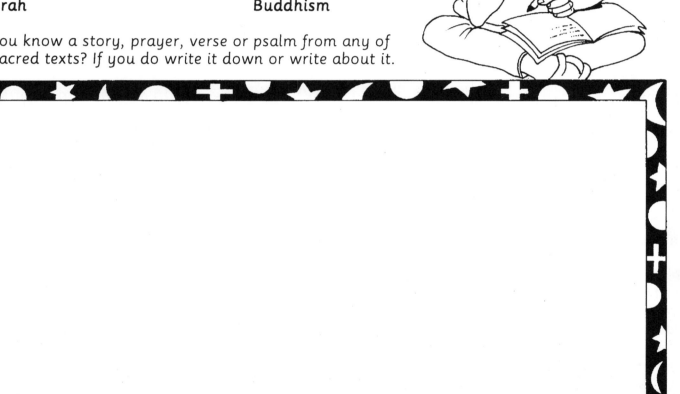

● Do you know a story, prayer, verse or psalm from any of these sacred texts? If you do write it down or write about it.

Get spaced out!

THEP LOU GHATE AS THEN DRED OX FOR DS HIRE

This says THE PLOUGH AT EAST HENDRED, OXFORDSHIRE.
It is a pub with a strange sign over the door.
Can you work out what the other sign says?

HERESTO PANDS PEN D ASOCI
AL HOU R INHAR M(LES SMIRT)
HA ND FUNLET FRIENDS
HIPRE IGN BE JUSTAN DK
INDAN DEVIL SPEAKOF NO NE

● Write a sign or a message and change the spaces so that it is
a bit like a code for your friends at school to try and decipher.

_____and

child

_____

helper(s)

_____

did this activity together

Grammar and language study

67

_____and

child

_____

helper(s)

_____

did this activity together

A name, not a number!

● Have a look at your birth certificate. Look after it, it tells the world you exist!

What other certificates and forms of identity do you have?

● Write a list. Make a facsimile (an identical copy) of one of them or make your own identity card and bring it to school. See if you can make it look so good that it fools your teacher!

impact WRITING HOMEWORK

Silent sections

'We might go in your umbrella', said Pooh.
'?'
'We might go in your umbrella', said Pooh.
'??'
'We might go in your umbrella', said Pooh.
'!!!!'
For suddenly Christopher Robin saw that they might.

From **Winnie the Pooh** by A.A. Milne

There are lots of ways that you can show the sound of silence in writing. Write a short story which includes a dialogue (a passage where two or more people are speaking to each other) and include some sections where you want your reader to read the silence.

To the helper:

● Suggest some examples of family life to provide ideas for writing the silent part of the dialogue, such as being ignored or being in a bad mood.
● Make suggestions about the kind of marks and symbols your child can use to express silence, such as dashes, dots, bubbles, question marks and exclamations.

This activity explores non-verbal vocalisations in written language. In class we will look at other examples of this technique in writing.

_____and

child

_____

helper(s)

_____

did this activity together

_____and

child

_____

helper(s)

_____

did this activity together

Matrices

A matrix is a table that shows information by using rows and columns. Some use both alphabetic (letters) and numeric (numbers) information like the football league tables for example:

	Played	Won	Drawn	Lost	Points
Manchester Utd	12	8	2	2	26
Newcastle Utd	11	7	1	3	22
Liverpool	12	7	1	4	22
Arsenal	12	6	2	4	20

● Devise a simple matrix for something going on at home. It could be a league table for who has washed up the most this week (or will Mum always win that league?)

Super-word!

'Super' comes from the Latin word meaning 'on top of, above or beyond'. The Romans brought Latin to Britain when they invaded in 43 AD. They left us with many words we now use in everyday speech. 'Super' is one which has changed a little to mean 'great' or 'really good' when used in speech. In writing it is used more often as a prefix in words like:

supernatural

supercharged

supersonic

● How many words can you think of that include the prefix 'super'? Make a list.

To the helper:

● 'Brainstorm' as many words as you can with 'super' in it and help your child with any spellings.
● You may get some ideas by skimming through newspapers or magazines especially in the advertisement sections.

This activity is intended to arouse interest in the origin of words, known as etymology and the development of the English language. In school we will be using dictionaries to further explore word origins and meanings as part of our work on language study and standard English.

_____and

child

_____

helper(s)

_____

did this activity together

impact WRITING HOMEWORK

_____and

child

_____

helper(s)

_____

did this activity together

Sub–stitute your pre–fix!

When the Romans brought their language, Latin, to Britain in 43 AD they gave us many words we now add on to words we use in our everyday speech. These 'add on' words are called prefixes when they come at the beginning of the word.

For example: **sub** is a Latin prefix meaning 'under, close to or towards'.

There are now hundreds of words in English with this Latin prefix such as:

submarine, **sub**stitute, **sub**ject and so on.

● How many words can you think of with **sub** as a prefix? Make a list.

pre is another **pre**fix meaning 'before' or 'in front of' from the Latin word 'prae'. There are hundreds of words in English with this Latin **pre**fix such as:

prepack, **pre**cast, **pre**dict and so on.

● How many words can you think of with **pre** as a prefix? Make a list.

Teachers' Notes
YEAR FIVE

American English Make an illustrated 'American-English dictionary' with the children's words. Write a cartoon strip with American characters or super-heroes using Americanisms. Write a funny extract from a play or film script where an American meets an English person and a muddle ensues because of misunderstandings. How well can children imitate American accents? Make an audio or visual recording of a sports or news event in American English.

Caxton's press Introduce the children to brief extracts of Shakespeare's English and spelling (perhaps linked to work on the Tudors). You could read the children some of Shakespeare's stories (re-told by people like Leon Garfield). Try some research on Caxton himself and his block printing techniques, and do some printing using various techniques. Make some 'gh' books using printing blocks. Look at the 'Caxton' computer software.

Gardening roots Gardening in school can be a rich source of scientific activity for children even if you only have room for window-boxes or pots. You could focus a whole project on growth around plants, fruit or vegetables looking at pollination,

germination, propagation, photosynthesis, growth rate, varieties and plant care. Parents can be a rich source of information and knowledge, not least free specimens!

How did it move? Discuss the prepositions the children have listed. Ask the children to draw pictures and label them with the prepositions they have used. Display them around the room. Show the children a hamster in a plastic rolling-ball toy and watch him move around the room (or show them a photo of one). Discuss what it would be like to be in the rolling-ball and ask the children to write a story as if they were in it. Where would they go? What different prepositions can they use? Read the children *I Houdini* by Lynn Reid Banks (Armada Books).

House for sale Ask the children to read out their descriptions and listen for the adjectives with the class. Discuss where the adjectives go to make the writing more interesting and see which were most common and most unique. Display the writing with adjectives highlighted or underlined next to the children's plans of their homes. Obtain actual house details from an estate agents and use these to compare/contrast with the children's work. Did the estate agent's descriptions match the type of descriptions the children made? Did the estate agent use any adjectives that the children did not?

Advert adjectives Look together at the products and descriptions that have been brought in. (Have a collection of old magazines and newspapers for use by children who have not completed the activity. They can look for adverts during any spare time.) Look for common adjectives and unique

ones. Tell the children to work individually, in pairs or small groups to design adverts for products of their choice (real or imaginary). The adverts could be posters, tape recorded broadcasts or even videos. Display (or play) them around the school. If the children have created their own product ask them to build a prototype or demonstration model.

Word builder Pin the children's lists to the wall or a washing line and ask them to read each other's lists. Did anyone find really unusual words? What words were most common? Tell the children to work in pairs to build compound words using: blue, book, horse or any other workable root words. Make a 'wall' for each root word used. Write the words on red card or sugar paper cut into brick shapes – root word on one brick, added word on another. See how many different compound words the children can find over the course of a week. Add any new words to the wall as they are discovered and reported, and see which root word gets the 'biggest wall'!

Missing apostrophes Explain the use of the apostrophe to indicate possession or belonging, before this goes home. When the pictures come back discuss the various uses of the apostrophe and the 's' including those which include an 's-apostrophe for example, 'Andrews' Hardware Store' or 'Cats' world'. Paint a street collage or class frieze of the local street using the information from their sheets. Make a display of 'Our Treasured Possessions' with labels: 'Tom's First Teddy Bear', 'Sarah's Favourite Doll' or 'Duane's Stamp Collection'. Make a book of the shops highlighting the possessive apostrophes.

Take your marks! Before you send the activity home, demonstrate some ideas for invented punctuation marks. Collect and display the ones the children bring back. Do a sound effects tape to substitute punctuation marks on a shared piece of writing. Organise some data collection to find out the distribution of full stops, commas, speech marks, colons, semi-colons and so on in a given piece of writing. Make pie charts or block graphs to show the usage.

Tell us a joke grandad! Make a collection of jokes from parents and grandparents and try to date them. What is the earliest joke you can trace? Analyse the language structure of the jokes the children bring in, help them to identify the 'feed', the 'tag' and the 'punch' lines. Have a class or assembly performance of *telling* the jokes (not reading them).

A rolling stone... Devise some role-play or drama activities which illustrate the proverbs, and perform them in class or assembly. Make a display or book collection of the stories. Try to collect some from other countries and languages. Ask the children to think of a personal experience that illustrates a well-known proverb.

Acronyms Use dictionaries to research abbreviations and acronyms from lists of organisations, charities and government bodies. Devise some dictionary games using this idea. Put the children in groups and time them against each other. The acronyms given are: North Atlantic Treaty Organisation; United Nations International Children's Emergency Fund; Royal Society for the Prevention of Accidents; Disc Operated System.

Common clichés Clichés are perhaps more common in spoken language, so ask the children to write in forms that reflect spoken language usage such as comic strips with speech bubbles or play scripts. These could be a source of humour, especially if you give them a theme setting such as 'Chicago gangland' and let the children perform them orally for the class or school assembly.

Up the totem-pole! Discuss why many groups of people and organisations are arranged in hierarchies, such as, families, schools and companies. Look at the way animal emblems are used by companies such as Lloyds Bank and Peugeot and by national sporting teams.

The rain in Spain This activity may provide some controversial discussion. Discuss the feelings expressed in the children's writing and set up class debates on the subject. Learn the song from 'My Fair Lady'. Read the poetry of writers who write in oral modes and in varieties of English such as Michael Rosen, John Agard and Grace Nichols. Discuss the ways they use language to represent different accents and dialects.

Animal adjectives Make some zigzag books of animals with their supposed attributes (see *Mr Gumpy's Outing* by John Burningham (Picture Puffin)), which could be used as 'reading books' for younger children in the school. Discuss how the names of animals (called nouns – for example, bull) can be converted in to adjectives (for example, bullish) and then in to verbs (for example, bully).

Feminine and masculine This activity will provoke a good deal of discussion about gender attitudes and behaviours. Ask the children to discuss (non-confrontationally) why they perceive objects and spaces to have a gender. Ask them to write about their perceptions: 'My favourite thing', or, 'My favourite space'. Have a look at other languages (especially with bilingual children in the class) and discuss the gender of various objects.

Alpha-bet translation Games and activities of writing in code can lead on from this activity. Invite the children to do some research on ancient systems of writing. Make Greek alphabet books and multilingual topic word books. Invite in local people who can speak and write in Greek to demonstrate.

Trade words Display a large Peters projection map (available from Oxfam Education) in the classroom and list the word collections against various countries and languages. Make bilingual dictionaries, glossaries or thesauri in zigzag book format with illustrations. Oxfam Education have very useful teaching materials on the political economy of the world trade. Contact them at: Oxfam Education, 274 Banbury Road, Oxford OX2 7DZ.

Cultural exchange Display a Peters projection map and find the relevant countries from where the words come. Put the children in groups and give them a card with the name of a country (each different). Ask them to generate as many words as they can think of that come from there. Make a display with lists of words and country flags or bilingual picture dictionaries.

The English variety Read the poetry of writers who write in dialects and varieties of English. Ask the children to write some short play-scripts from their favourite TV soaps including their favourite characters, written in the non-standard variety. They can act them using the appropriate accents. Make tapes of the children speaking to illustrate the variety of accents and speech patterns amongst them.

Braille Demonstrate the activity before sending it home. Make a Braille Alphabet Book. Ask the children to learn the entire alphabet and encourage them to 'write' to each other in class using Braille! Invite a fluent Braille reader in to demonstrate other aspects of the skill. Explore other sign systems such as British Sign Language, see page 63.

Rebuses Demonstrate this activity before you send it home. Try it with themes from class topics and explore other language play like word squares, palindromes, acrostics and crosswords. See *The Cambridge Encyclopaedia of Language,* D Crystal (Cambridge University Press), pages 64–65 for more ideas. 'Translations' are 1. Excuse me; 2. Split second timing; 3. Smallpox infection.

Parlez–vous Jabberwocky? Read the whole of *Jabberwocky* (Lewis Carroll, Barefoot Books) to the class. Find other nonsense literature for them to translate. Can the children think of any 'rules' for writing nonsense language? Compare the children's translations and discuss their interpretations of the poem. Ask the children to choose a favourite poem and turn it into a nonsense poem.

American English

In 1828 the American lexicographer (dictionary maker) Noah Webster wanted to make American English a different language and published his now famous dictionary to try and promote the idea. He simplified spellings and changed words. Not all of his ideas caught on.

● Find out what words Americans use for these:

a pavement _____

petrol _____

biscuits _____

autumn _____

sweets _____

trousers _____

the boot of a car _____

jam _____

● These are words which Americans use. What words do we use for them?

a freeway _____

a tub _____

a truck _____

jello _____

a bathroom _____

an eraser _____

a garbage can _____

a hood _____

_____and

child

_____

helper(s)

_____

did this activity together

_____and

child

_____

helper(s)

_____

did this activity together

Caxton's press

William Caxton introduced the printing press in to England in 1476. He had learned about printing techniques in Europe, particularly in a place called Flanders (now Belgium) where Flemish speakers used the letters 'gh' in many words. When he returned to England he introduced many new words in to Old English spelling by adding a 'g' or a 'gh'.

● Can you turn these Old English spellings into Caxton's English?

DAILY POST

riht _____

toh _____

ruh _____

sihth _____

boht _____

thurh _____

miht _____

niht _____

flyht _____

Gardening roots

Plants, bulbs and shrubs all have Latin names (so that everyone all over the world can call them by the same name) and they also have 'common' or 'popular' names (which they are known by in particular countries).

Do you know the difference between a bulb and a flower, a fruit and a vegetable or a hardy perennial and an annual?

Do you have a local park, municipal garden or allotment where there is a shrubbery, rose garden or vegetable patch?

● If you have a garden, balcony or window-box find out the names of the plants, bulbs, fruit or vegetables that grow in it.

● Match up the Latin names of these well known bulbs and plants with their common names:

Sweet Pea

Dianthus   Carnation

Tulip

Narcissus   Primrose

Daffodil

Galanthus   Lathyrus

Tulipa

Snowdrop   Primula

● If you have any plants at home, do a close observational drawing of your favourite one, label it with its name and bring it in to school.

To the helper:

● You should be able to sort some of these by the similarity of their names.
● For others, you could use a dictionary or any gardening books or magazines you may have. Better still, consult a neighbour or relative who has an interest in gardening.

This activity focuses on the use of proper nouns and familiarises children with the convention of Latin naming and 'popular' naming that is in use in many professions and walks of life such as biology, horticulture and medicine.

_____and

child

_____

helper(s)

_____

did this activity together

_____and

child

_____

helper(s)

_____

did this activity together

How did it move?

● You will need a small ball or a toy car. Drop it on the floor and watch it roll. Ask your partner to describe the path which the toy took. What words did they use to describe where the toy went?

● With your partner write a short story to describe where the toy went as it moved.

impact WRITING HOMEWORK

House for sale

Imagine that you want to sell your home.

● Write a description of your home to make it sound really interesting. Make sure you include adjectives in your writing so your home sounds really special!

_____and

child

_____

helper(s)

_____

did this activity together

_____and

child

_____

helper(s)

_____

did this activity together

Advert adjectives

● Look at some adverts with your helper. They can be on TV, radio or in newspapers and magazines. Look at the words used to describe the items being advertised. Are they larger, stronger, faster?

● Choose some and write down the name of the product, what it is and the adjectives or describing words used. If you are looking at printed adverts ask permission to cut them out and bring them into school.

impact WRITING HOMEWORK

Word builder

- Think about the word: foot.

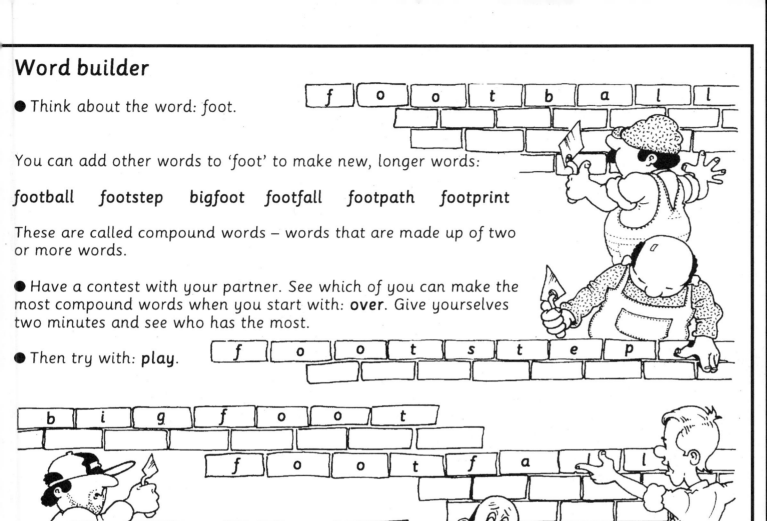

You can add other words to 'foot' to make new, longer words:

football   footstep   bigfoot   footfall   footpath   footprint

These are called compound words – words that are made up of two or more words.

- Have a contest with your partner. See which of you can make the most compound words when you start with: **over**. Give yourselves two minutes and see who has the most.

- Then try with: **play**.

To the helper:

- Encourage your child to think of as many words as possible reminding them that the root word (the word that all the words are built from) can go at the front or back of the new word.

Building compound words expands children's vocabulary and encourages them to widen their thought processes. We have been looking at the formation of different words and will be building more compound words in class.

_____and

child

_____

helper(s)

_____

did this activity together

_____and

child

_____

helper(s)

_____

did this activity together

Missing apostrophes

We often use apostrophes before an 's' if we are trying to show that something belongs to someone, like this:

'Patel's Foodstores'
'Greenberg's Opticians'
'Westlake's Chemists'
'Virdee's Newsagents'

Many of your local shops will leave out the apostrophe and sometimes even the 's' as well. Why do you think this is?

● Draw a picture to show some of the shops in your local high street. Write in the shop signs with an apostrophe and the 's' in each case. These are called 'possessive apostrophes' because they show possession or ownership of property or belongings.

Take your marks!

● Invent your own punctuation marks to express the ideas in your latest story.

● Give your punctuation marks names, for example:

a 'Sadlamation Mark' to express sadness at a sad point in your story.

To the helper:

● Talk about and list all the punctuation marks you know of and what they do to help us read pieces of writing with pauses and emphases.

● Use your imagination to design some alternative punctuation marks for the needs of your child's particular story.

Identifying the need for punctuation is the first task in learning about it. Curiously, making up some alternative punctuation marks will actually help your child remember the originals and their uses.

_____and

child

_____

helper(s)

_____

did this activity together

_____and

child

_____

helper(s)

_____

did this activity together

Tell us a joke grandad!

● Ask mum or dad, or even better, gran or grandad to tell you a joke which they used to tell when they were a child.

● Write it down and ask them to recall what year that was (approximately).

Is it different from the jokes you know nowadays?

● Write one of your own favourite jokes down too, and bring them both into school.

impact WRITING HOMEWORK

A rolling stone...

'A rolling stone gathers no moss' is a well-known proverb and most people know what it means.

● Make up a short story that expresses the meaning of the proverb. It doesn't have to be long. Ask your helper to help you and when you have finished read it through together. Bring it into school and listen to other people's proverb stories.

Do you know any proverbs from other countries that can be translated into English?

To the helper:

● Explain that the rolling stone proverb is often used to refer to people who don't like to stay in the same place or do the same thing for very long.
● Help with ideas for a story that will illustrate the point of the proverb.

Proverbs are a fascinating insight into the oral and social history of a language. A proverb can have meaning in many different contexts and can encompass hundreds of stories. In school we will explore their meanings and use them as a source of ideas for stories.

_____and

child

_____

helper(s)

_____

did this activity together

_____and

child

_____

helper(s)

_____

did this activity together

Acronyms

Acronyms are words that have been made up from the initial letters of the phrase they refer to, like this:

POSH – 'Port Outward Starboard Home' – this is a word meaning 'upper class' or 'very smart and stylish' but it seems that it originated from the time when the East India Steamship Company ran a passenger service to India and the Far East. The most expensive cabins were reserved for those which were shaded from the full heat of the sun on the Port side (left side) of the ship going East and the Starboard side (right side) of the ship on the leg returning West. Only the wealthiest people could afford these cabins and so they became known as 'POSH'.

● Do you know any acronyms?
Write down as many as you can think of.

● Work out what some of these stand for:

NATO _____

_____

UNICEF _____

_____

RoSPA _____

_____

DOS _____

_____

impact WRITING HOMEWORK

Common clichés

A cliché is an over-used or 'hackneyed' phrase. But the word cliché derives from a French word for a printing block used to repeat common words and phrases, also known as 'stereotypes'.

● Write down some clichés that you and your family use or some that you have heard used on TV, film or video.

To the helper:

● Footballers being interviewed on television are often a good source of clichés: 'It's a game of two halves'; 'The ball came across and there it was in the back of the net', for example.
● Think of some clichés used by politicians, soap opera characters or movie stars.

This activity is intended to help children understand various aspects of language use and how such things as clichés can be both meaningful and meaningless at the same time.

_____and

child

_____

helper(s)

_____

did this activity together

_____and

child

_____

helper(s)

_____

did this activity together

Up the totem-pole!

Totems derive from the culture of Native North Americans. They are images of animals which are emblems for individuals of family clans. These are arranged vertically on a pole to represent the order or hierarchy within the clan (so the clan leader's emblem will be at the top and the most junior member's emblem will be at the bottom).

● On a piece of paper, draw a picture of a totem-pole for your family and write a short explanation below to go with it.

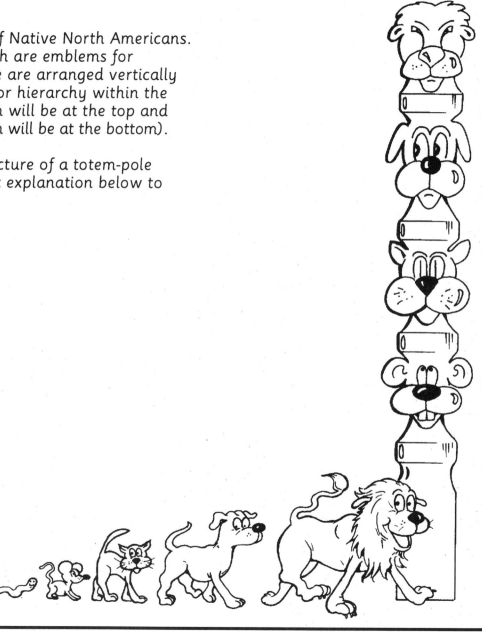

The rain in Spain

In George Bernard Shaw's famous play Pygmalion, Professor Higgins tries an experiment to turn the speech of a flower-selling Cockney girl in to that of an upper class lady. He gives her elocution lessons making her repeat the phrase 'The rain in Spain falls mainly on the plain'.

Has there ever been a time when you have been made to feel that the way you speak is not 'correct' or 'proper'?

● Have you ever felt embarrassed about the way you, a friend or a member of your family speak? Write about it.

To the helper:

● Discuss with your child about the varieties of ways that people speak using different accents (pronunciation) and dialects (vocabulary and grammar).
● Discuss whether you think there are correct or incorrect ways of speaking.

This activity looks at attitudes about language variety. In school we will examine accents and dialects more closely as part of our scheme of work on language study and standard English.

_____and

child

_____

helper(s)

_____

did this activity together

Animal adjectives

Fishy   Bullish   Catty   Piggish

These adjectives (words which describe a person, place or thing) are all derived from animals and their characteristics.

● How many can you think of? Write them down.

Feminine and masculine

Many names have feminine and masculine versions:

Nicola – Nicholas
Lesley – Leslie
Roberta – Robert

● Write down as many feminine and masculine versions of names as you can think of.

Many languages have genders for the names of other things. For example in French a hat (un chapeau) is masculine whereas a jacket (une veste) is feminine. In other languages, some things have no gender and are neutral.

● If the English language had genders what gender would you make the following items (feminine, masculine or neutral):

a car _____

an apple _____

a pub _____

a supermarket _____

a bicycle _____

a strawberry _____

a library _____

a tree _____

a banana _____

a double-decker bus _____

a flower _____

a pineapple _____

a computer _____

a grape _____

a football stadium _____

To the helper:

● Help with spellings of unfamiliar names.
● Discuss whether you think the objects themselves have feminine or masculine characteristics or whether you think we just attach our attitudes to them.

This activity uses discussion of familiar objects to help children prepare for aspects of language study which they will meet later on, such as the study of the grammar of foreign languages. It also helps them reflect on the particular characteristics of the English language.

_____and

child

_____

helper(s)

_____

did this activity together

_____and

child

_____

helper(s)

_____

did this activity together

Alpha-bet translation

The alphabet was invented to save us from having to draw pictures every time we wanted to write something down. Instead of representing objects in pictures, alphabet writing could represent the sounds of our voices. The Phoenicians (in what is now Lebanon) were the first to invent an alphabet. The Greeks added vowels and later the Romans adapted it to the one that we know today.

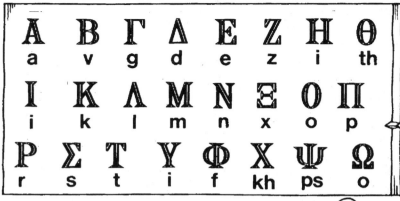

● Try to translate these words from Greek in to Roman.
(Note that in Greek the ΜΠ is used for a 'B' sound.)

ΦΟΤΜΠΟΔ _____   ΦΟΤΟΓΠΑΦ _____

ΒΙΔΕΟ _____   ΤΑΞΙ _____

● Try to translate these Roman alphabet words in to Greek.

television _____

radio _____

athlete _____

Olympics _____

● Write a phrase in Greek to bring back to school for your friends to decipher!

Trade words

Over the centuries new words have entered the English language through commerce and trade from around the world. Many of these words have become so common that we now use them everyday. Words such as tea (from China), tomato (from Central America), pyjamas (from India), orange (from the Middle East) and potato (from North America).

● Make a list of words that you think may have entered English through the centuries of trade and commerce with the rest of the world.

● List them with the countries you think the words may have come from.

Make a guess if you do not know for sure.

To the helper:

● Go to the fridge and food cupboard and look through all the items of food and drink you have.
● Do the same with your clothes, furniture and other household items.

This activity is intended to arouse interest in the diverse roots of modern English and explore the origins of words, known as etymology. We will look more closely at word origins using dictionaries in school.

_____and

child

_____

helper(s)

_____

did this activity together

_____and

child

_____

helper(s)

_____

did this activity together

Cultural exchange

Many common words that we use everyday have entered English through the exchange of the language and culture of television, films, books, art and through people travelling to different countries on holiday.

Words such as kebab, brochure, reggae, judo, pizza, macho and vodka have been introduced.

● Make a list of words that you think may have come in to English usage this way.

● Write a short story using as many of them as you can as part of the events and plot.

● Draw a picture including as many of the items as you can and label each one.

The English variety

English has a rich diversity of accents and dialects all around the world. But you don't have to go to the other side of the world to hear them. Turn on your TV and listen out for different accents.

● Try to list as many people as you can from TV, radio, video or film who speak English with one of these accents:

West Yorkshire _____

Liverpool 'Scouse' _____

Scots Glaswegian _____

Australian 'Strine' _____

American New York _____

Belfast Irish _____

American Southern Drawl _____

Dublin Irish _____

Birmingham 'Brum' _____

London 'Cockney' _____

South African _____

'Queen's English' _____

Jamaican _____

Newcastle 'Geordie' _____

Lancashire/Manchester _____

Scots Edinburgh _____

To the helper:

● A good source of ideas for this activity will be the TV soaps but you may also want to think of pop stars and movie actors.

This activity is intended to arouse interest in the rich diversity of English in Britain and around the world. In school we will look more closely at language variety as part of our scheme of work on language study and standard English.

_____and

child

_____

helper(s)

_____

did this activity together

Grammar and language study   95

_____and

child

_____

helper(s)

_____

did this activity together

Braille

Braille is a system of written language devised for blind people. The symbols are of a maximum of six raised dots shaped in to a rectangle embossed on paper.

Readers of Braille read by running their fingers along the page to feel the dots.

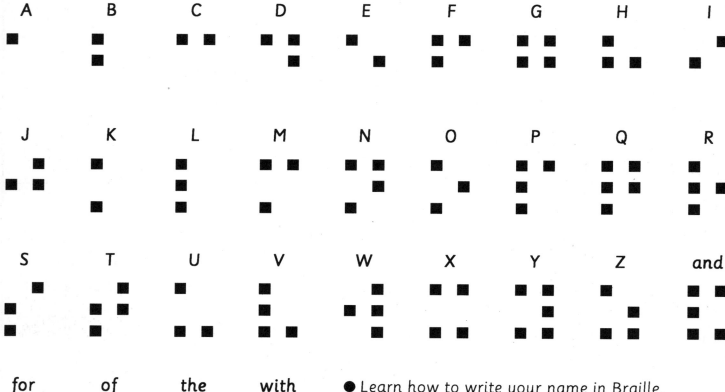

● Learn how to write your name in Braille.

impact WRITING HOMEWORK

Rebuses

A rebus mixes letters and pictures to make words and sentences.

Like this:

YY U R   Too wise you are

YY U B   Too wise you be

I C U R   I see you are

YY 4 ME   Too wise for me

● Here are some to try for yourself:

1. XQQ ME! _____

2. Timing Tim ing _____

3. FECpoxTION _____

● Now make one of your own!

To the helper:

● You need a bit of lateral thinking for these!

● Start by deciding on the words you want to try and 'rebus' and then think of objects that you can draw a picture of, or words and letters that sound like your idea. It's a bit like charades on paper!

This activity explores one of the more curious and playful aspects of language, the phenomenon of rebuses.

_____and

child

_____

helper(s)

_____

did this activity together

To the helper:

● What do some of the words remind you of? What are the *slithy toves* and why did they *gyre* and *gimble*?

● Don't worry, it doesn't mean anything! It is a nonsense poem, so you can let your imagination run free and make up the meanings when you 'translate' this hilarious and classic piece of children's literature.

This activity gives children an opportunity to 'translate' a 'foreign language', in this case a nonsense poem. But the translation and interpretation skills involved are real.

_____and

child

_____

helper(s)

_____

did this activity together

Parlez–vous Jabberwocky?

Twas brillig, and the slithy toves
Did gyre and gimble in the wabe:
All mimsy were the borogroves,
And the mome raths outgrabe.

These are the opening lines from
Lewis Carroll's *Jabberwocky*.
But what does it mean?

● Translate it if you can!

impact WRITING HOMEWORK

Teachers' Notes
Y E A R   S I X

Headline alliteration Keep some newspapers handy for children who have not completed the activity. Make a display of headlines that have been brought in, and ask the children to write articles to accompany these headlines. Publish them in a newspaper format using a word processor and a double column layout, or use a desktop publishing package. Encourage the children to add suitable illustrations/photos and captions; distribute finished copies to other children.

School day conversation You may want to send a sheet of lined paper home for this activity. Back in school ask the children to swap sheets and read each other's work. Let the children read them in two parts to re-enact the conversation, and use them as a basis for a class play or puppet show (write a script by combining conversations and suggestions for additions from the children). Fold a sheet of lined paper in half down the centre. On the left side show dialogue and on the right show actions, sound effects and prop requirements. Produce the plays or puppet shows in small groups. Record the dialogue so the children can focus on the actions and sound effects that are needed.

Talk about it! Compare the stories which the children have written with the comics. How are they different? How are they the same? What were the main changes they had to make? Display the writing and the comic side by side or in a double page book format. Tell the children to find a partner (or assign partners) and give each pair a suitable comic strip. In their pairs ask them to write the comic in a narrative form. Encourage them to add describing language and linking sentences and phrases to describe the comic illustrations.

Conjunction junction Ask the children to read out their favourite pair of sentences and the three joined sentences. With the class discuss how the meaning changes. Make a three-flap book: take sheets of A4 paper or card and mark them in thirds. On the top third write the first half of the sentences, on the middle third write the different conjunctions and on the bottom third the last part of the sentences. Cut the paper along the marks and bind them using a binding machine (or staple or sew them together). Let the children read the book making different sentences by combining the different sentence sections and using various conjunctions. Discuss the differences between the sentences when different conjunctions are used.

Negative prefixes Write each prefix in large print in the centre of sheets of sugar paper. Ask the children (a few at a time) to add their new words to the sheets checking that their word does not already appear on the page. Display the papers around the room and encourage the children to add new words. Check the lists from time to time to see which prefix has the greatest number of words. Attempt to use these 'new' words in the course of everyday conversation and class/group discussion.

Say it again Ask the children to read out their altered sentences and the originals. As a class, discuss the new meanings and why one meaning may be better than another. Explain to the children that one form is active language, where blame or ownership is made evident, and that the other form is passive language, where the cause is left open and ambiguous. Discuss when these different forms are used – trouble at playtime, broken items at home or school for example. Display the sentences on a washing line with the original meaning on one side of a card and the altered form on the other.

Sound effect punctuation Give the children a few minutes to rehearse their readings and then ask them to perform them for the class. See if the other children can guess what punctuation has been used in each passage. Ask the children to record their readings for others to listen to.

What did you do today? Look at the words which the children have used. Explain that conjunctions join sentences together and that relative adverbs help to fix a particular event to a specific activity or time. Write stories using a variety of conjunctions and relative adverbs that relate time to events.

What's in a name? Discuss with the children the names they have found and their possible meanings. Find a book that gives name origins. See if any staff members know the origin of their family name and share this information with the children. Illustrate and display the names.

When did it happen? Tell the children to practise their conversations with a partner and then to read them to the class and let the class guess what tense, past or present is being used. Working individually or in pairs tell the children to change the conversation so that they are talking about something that will not happen until tomorrow (in the future). Discuss with the whole class how the future tense is different from the other two. Put the conversations into a book with a page for each tense.

Recipe for disaster Explore the frequency of usage of metaphors in our everyday speech to point out how much we rely on them. Investigate what other issues or themes can be metaphorically illustrated by a recipe. What other forms of writing can be used to illustrate the theme of disaster? A menu, a manual, a catalogue? Try different ideas and see which ones have the most effect.

Singular or plural? Demonstrate this activity with some examples before sending it home. Make class lists of categories of 'singular, plural and same for both' and display them. Set the children tasks of dictionary activities looking for the plurals of singulars and the singulars of plurals. Make games between groups of children with these activities, and time them to improve dictionary skills.

Signs and symbols Discuss the variety and meanings of the signs and symbols which the children bring in. Compare these to dictionary definitions. Look at the symbols on computer keyboards. Ask the children to invent 'Smiley Faces' using keyboard symbols. Play 'Keyboard Bingo'; make some blank templates of a keyboard with blank spaces for letter and symbol keys. Hold up cards one by one with different letters and keyboard symbols on and ask the children to draw them in the correct blank spaces of the keyboard.

Have you got an 'ology? Look at the beginnings of the words and explore their meanings for example: psycho, gynaec, soci, bi, and so on. Make word-slides (two pieces of attached card, one with a window cut out and *ology* written beside it. Write the word beginnings on an insert and slide them up and down behind the window to make different words visible).

French English Sort the children's lists by putting the abbreviation OF next to the words they think are Norman (Old French). Discuss the meanings of the words using good dictionaries; look for the abbreviation OF for Old French at the end of the definition. Devise a range of dictionary activities around the list such as putting the lists in alphabetical order or finding other related words. Teach the children how to use a Children's Thesaurus.

O Romeo, Romeo Make a collection of puns and discuss their different meanings. Look more closely at the way Shakespeare used them in some of the more accessible plays for older primary children (see school editions of *A Midsummer Night's Dream* or *Macbeth*). Make up some funny puns and put them in a 'Joke Book of Puns'. (For example: Burying the Headteacher in the school playground is a matter of grave concern.)

Long live Welsh? Discuss with the children contemporary issues about language in Britain and around the world. Discuss how Welsh almost became extinct. Encourage the children to do some research about the Welsh language today and the campaign to revive it. They could make some English-Welsh word books, and if you know a local Welsh speaker invite them in to talk to the children.

English around the world Plot all the countries on a Peters projection map in class. Categorise them by L^1 or L^2. Can you find out approximately how many people speak English as a daily language? Provide each child with a photocopy of a world map outline to take home to accompany the sheet.

World languages Make a graph and pie chart to show the proportions of different languages spoken. Assign a colour to each language and colour a blank map of the world according to languages spoken. Discuss why certain languages are spoken in particular parts of the world, for example: Portuguese in Brazil. The correct order for the world's most widely spoken languages is 1) Chinese (about 800m); 2) English (300m); 3) Spanish (225m); 4) Hindi (200m); 5) Russian (150m); 6) Bengali (125m); 7) Arabic (120m); 8) Portuguese (105m); 9 & 10) Japanese and German (100m each). Provide each child with a photocopy of a world map outline to to take home to accompany the sheet.

Multilingual Britain Display a large map of the UK and plot the towns, cities and regions with their various languages. Make some simple mulitlingual books on the themes of colours, foods, toys and games. Make some signs in different languages for the school or classroom. Arabic (Kensington), Bengali (Tower Hamlets), Chinese (Soho), Cornish (Cornwall), Gaelic (Scottish highlands and islands), Greek (Haringey, Birmingham), Gujerati (Wembley), Hindi (Birmingham), Punjabi (Southall, Leicester, Bradford, Birmingham), Spanish (Paddington), Turkish (Stoke Newington), Ukranian (Halifax), Urdu (Bradford, Birmingham), Welsh (Wales), Yiddish (Stamford Hill), Yoruba (Hackney). Provide each child with a photocopy of a UK map outline to take home.

Chinese ideas If possible invite someone in to class who can demonstrate writing in Chinese using brush and ink and to explain translations and interpretations. Encourage the children to invent a symbol to stand for their name (the rock star, Prince did this). Tell them to focus on the physical attributes or personal characteristics. Make a display of the children's writing with dual language Chinese-English books and artefacts.

From Russia Plenty of games and activities of writing in code can be investigated using the Russian alphabet. Try writing names, a joke or a riddle in Russian. Make a passport in Russian, Russian alphabet books and multilingual topic word books. Ask the children to do some research on different systems of writing. Look at the different fonts on word processors such as 'dingbats'.

Spelling mistake identity parade This activity helps children develop the visual awareness needed for editing and proofing writing. As a follow-up devise some activities where they have to add errors to a passage of writing which their class partners have to identify by type.

Car mechanic Make a display of a car and its engine and label it. Bring in some car manuals and information books. If you can, try to organise a visit by a car mechanic (perhaps a parent), to explain some of the simple parts and workings of a car engine, using a real one if possible.

Green fingers Gardening in school can be a rich source of scientific activity for children even if you only have room for window-boxes or pots. Make a project looking at pollination, germination, propagation, photosynthesis, growth rate, varieties and care. Parents can be a rich source of information and knowledge, not least free specimens!

World-wide proverbs Before you send this activity home ask the children to learn at least one of the proverbs and its meaning, so they can introduce it to their parent or helper. Make a class book of the stories they write. Look at other collections of traditional tales from different cultures and countries that use proverbs as the central feature of the tale.

Name gamer! Anagram me! Demonstrate this activity before you send it home. They may find it too difficult to do using all the letters at first. Try it with themes from class topics and explore other language play like word squares, palindromes, acrostics, rebuses and crosswords. See *The Cambridge Encyclopaedia of Language*, D Crystal (Cambridge University Press) pages 64–65 for more ideas on this.

Headline alliteration

Alliteration is when a group of words all start with the same letter, like this:

'sing a song of sixpence' or 'cool, calm and collected'.

Newspapers quite often use alliteration in their headlines and photo captions.

● Look through a newspaper to find some examples of alliteration. Cut them out (be sure to ask permission first!) and bring them in to school.

● Try to make up some headlines of your own using alliteration. Make them funny!

THE BLURB
Monday 14th. October 1996
10p

PLANT PROTECTION PLAN

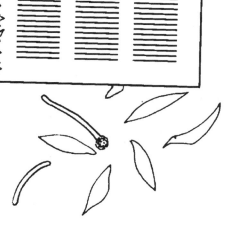

Daft Doreen daily drags Digger the dog down the ditch dismantling the dainty daisy on the descent.

To the helper:

● Talk with your child about the alliterative words used.
● Were any 'funny' or 'unusual' words used? Did the author make up or change any words so the alliteration would work?

This activity focuses the children on different word forms and how they may be linked through alliteration. We will be discussing the alliterations that are brought in and displaying them. We will also be writing articles of our own to match the headlines brought in from home.

_____and

child

_____

helper(s)

_____

did this activity together

School day conversation

● Have a short conversation with your helper at home about your day at school. Write down what each of you says.

Every time a new person speaks, start on a new line. Don't forget to use speech marks and say who is speaking.

Your writing will look something like this:

'We made masks today,' said Cagdas.
'How did you do that?' asked Gran.
'We put cream on our faces so the plaster wouldn't stick. Then we used art rock to make the mask,' said Cagdas.

● Try to record what you have said for about two minutes.

Talk about it!

● Look at a comic book or a comic strip in your local paper. Choose a section that has quite a few speech bubbles in it.

● Rewrite the comic in story form, using speech marks and proper punctuation. You may need to add other sentences to explain the actions which are taking place. Explain to your helper what changes you have made and why.

● Bring your completed story and the comic into school. Don't forget to ask permission to bring in the comic or cut up the paper!

To the helper:

● Help your child choose a comic that has enough conversation to make a short story. Remind your child that each time a new person speaks, they need to start a new line.

● Help in adding any extra information to describe the actions.

We are practising the use of punctuation in direct speech. We are also looking at different forms of writing and comparing them. We will be comparing the short stories and the comics to see which form gives more detail and how art work takes the place of the written word.

_____and

child

_____

helper(s)

_____

did this activity together

_____and

child

_____

helper(s)

_____

did this activity together

Conjunction junction

Conjunctions are words that join two or more small sentences to make one big sentence. Some common conjunctions are: so, but and because.

We could use them to join these sentences:
Carmalita was naughty. She was sent to bed.

Carmalita was naughty **so** *she was sent to bed.*
Carmalita was naughty **but** *she was sent to bed.*
Carmalita was naughty **because** *she was sent to bed.*

How are the meanings different for the three sentences?

● With your helper make up three pairs of sentences and join each pair using: so, but and because.

Negative prefixes

A negative tells the reader that something is **not** going to happen, that the writer does **not** enjoy something or that there are **no** members in a group.

We can make adjectives (words that describe people, places and things) negative by adding certain prefixes to them. A prefix is a group of letters that we add to the beginning of a word to change its meaning.

For example: I am happy. I am **un**happy.
Here 'un' is a prefix that makes words negative. Some other prefixes that make words negative are im, mis and dis.

● Using these four prefixes make a list of as many negatives as you can:

un-   im-   mis-   dis-

See who can think of the most, you, or your partner!

To the helper:

● Have a piece of paper each, split it into four columns with the prefixes at the top of each. Encourage your child to add the prefix to different words and check to see if the word makes sense.
● Compare lists to see who has the most original words. Which prefix was easiest to create new words with?

The use of prefixes is an important word-building skill. It is useful for expanding children's vocabulary and adding variety to their written work.

_____and

child

_____

helper(s)

_____

did this activity together

_____and

child

_____

helper(s)

_____

did this activity together

Say it again

● Look at this sentence: **I lost the remote control.**

How could you say it differently?
How about: **The remote control has been lost.**

How is the meaning different for the two sentences.
How is it the same?

● Can you change these sentences in the same way:

The dog chewed the newspaper.

_____

_____

_____

She broke your coffee mug.

_____

_____

_____

He washed the dinner dishes.

_____

_____

_____

● On the back of the sheet write two sentences of your own and change their meaning.

impact WRITING HOMEWORK

Sound effect punctuation

● Choose a short passage from your reading book, or a story you have written yourself. The passage should include as many different punctuation marks as possible (! . ' ? " ,).

● Make up a sound effect for each different punctuation mark. Try to make the sound resemble the punctuation mark.
For example, a full stop could be a **pop!**

● Read your story out using your sound effects for the punctuation.

● Practise several times so you can read your passage out to the class.

Make it sound **FUN!**

To the helper:

● Choose some writing with a lot of different types of punctuation; a younger child's book for example. Alternatively, write a short passage with your child.
● Discuss what sound each different punctuation mark could have. The sound could be related to its shape or its effect on the sentence.

We are studying punctuation and how it is used within writing. We have also been working on making our reading more expressive. This activity reinforces the use of punctuation and helps develop expression.

_____and

child

_____

helper(s)

_____

did this activity together

_____and

child

_____

helper(s)

_____

did this activity together

What did you do today?

● Think about what you did today.

● Write a list of five things that happened.

For example: **I watched TV.**

_____

_____

_____

_____

● Now think about **when** they happened.

I watched TV as I ate my dinner.

A conjunction (as) joins these ideas and gives the reader a better idea of when things happened.

● Write a sentence for each of your five things that happened and then use a conjunction to tell when it happened.

What's in a name?

Have you ever wondered where people's surnames (last names) come from?

The Jolly family must have had a relative that was lots of fun to have around!

The Kingsman family had an ancestor that worked for the king.

Someone in the Carter's past made and repaired carts and wagons.

The Johnson family were named after the son of John.

● Think about your family name and what it may mean.

● See if any relative knows where it comes from or try to work it out. Write down what you find out.

● Think of friends' names or look through the phone book to find other names that give a clue as to where the names originated.

To the helper:

● If you know the origin of your family name, or of the names of any relatives explain them to your child.

● Look through the phone book. Try to think of jobs, places, descriptions, characteristics or relatives that may have been the origin of family names you find there.

We have been looking at word origins. We will be discussing possible origins for names of children within the class and other names that have been discovered.

_____and

child

_____

helper(s)

_____

did this activity together

_____and

child

_____

helper(s)

_____

did this activity together

When did it happen?

● With your helper write a short conversation between two people. It can be about a trip to the shops, a football match, your favourite TV programme – anything you like. Write the conversation as if it were happening **NOW**, as you are writing it. Be sure to use speech marks whenever possible!

● Now change the conversation so that what you are talking about has already happened (is in the past).

impact WRITING HOMEWORK

Recipe for disaster

● Write a recipe for disaster. It could be a natural disaster, a civil war in our own country or a social evil like racism.

● What are the ingredients? What are the measures? What is the method for cooking up the mixture?

_____and

child

_____

helper(s)

_____

did this activity together

_____and

child

_____

helper(s)

_____

did this activity together

Singular or plural?

Singular means one, plural means more than one. But in which category would you put the following items?

● Write them under these column headings: **singular** or **plural** or **same for both.**

trousers
aircraft
Greek
mouse
Japanese
medium
spaghetti
bacteria
zombie
furniture
media
accommodation
moose
data
datum

singular	plural	same for both

impact WRITING HOMEWORK

Signs and symbols

In some writing symbols such as Chinese, a single symbol represents an idea.

For example, '木' means 'tree' and '林' means 'wood'. These signs are called ideographs. We have these ideographs in English too.

● Write down in words the names of these symbols, where they are used in the English writing system and explain what they mean:

a) £ _____

b) ? _____

c) ! _____

d) & _____

e) ♥ _____

Can you think of any others?

Mathematics has a writing system all of its own.

● Write down in words the names of these symbols and what you think they mean:

a) = _____

b) + _____

c) × _____

d) % _____

e) – _____

Do you know any others?

_____and

child

_____

helper(s)

_____

did this activity together

Have you got an 'ology?

A suffix is an 'added on' end to a word.

The suffix 'ology' comes from the ancient Greek 'logos' meaning 'the study of a word'.

Many words in modern English now use these Greek suffixes, for example psych**ology**, gynaec**ology** and so on.

● How many words do you know with 'ology' as a suffix? Make a list.

● Can you think of other words or phrases with this Greek root 'logos'? Words like cata**log**ue (meaning a list in alphabetical order) or 'Captain's **Log**' (meaning a record of a ship's passage) or 'to **log** on' (meaning to access the language of a computer). Make a list of these too.

impact WRITING HOMEWORK

French English

In 1066 the Normans came from northern France and invaded and conquered England. They took over the government and the royal courts and many words we use in modern English today come from that time, words such as:

government, nation, justice, court, verdict, legal and so on.

● How many other words to do with **government** can you think of? Make a list here.

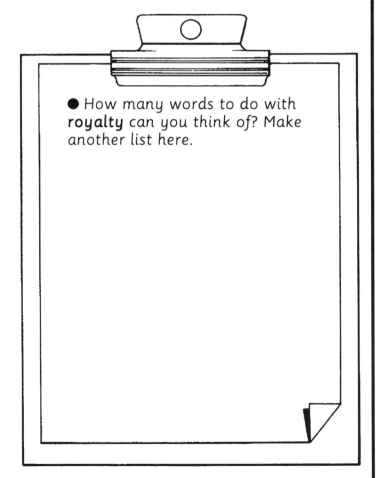

● How many words to do with **royalty** can you think of? Make another list here.

_____and

child

_____

helper(s)

_____

did this activity together

_____and

child

_____

helper(s)

_____

did this activity together

O Romeo, Romeo

In Elizabethan times William Shakespeare amused his audience by using words that have the same sound and often the same spelling but different meanings. These are called puns.

● Find the puns in this extract from Romeo and Juliet and explain as many as you can.

Romeo: …You have dancing shoes with nimble soles,
I have a soul of lead that so stakes me to the ground I cannot move.

Mercutio: You are a lover, borrow Cupid's wings, And soar with them above a common bound.

Romeo: I am too sore enpierced with this shaft to soar with his light feathers, and so bound I cannot bound a pitch above dull woe: Under love's heavy burden do I sink.

Romeo and Juliet fell in love at first sight but their love was 'star crossed'.

Do you know what happened to Romeo and Juliet and why?

impact WRITING HOMEWORK

Long live Welsh?

Before the Romans invaded Britain in 43AD most people in Britain spoke Celtic languages such as Welsh, Gaelic and Cornish. Over the centuries these languages have sadly almost died out. Although Welsh is now once again thriving, during the last century children who spoke Welsh in school in Wales were punished for doing so. If they were heard speaking Welsh rather than English (which they were told was a superior language), they would be beaten or fined and forced to wear a piece of wood hung around their neck with the letters 'WN' engraved on it, meaning 'Welsh Not'.

Why do you think this was?

● Write a story imagining that you are a Welsh child at school in the last century.

_____and

child

_____

helper(s)

_____

did this activity together

_____and

child

_____

helper(s)

_____

did this activity together

English around the world

English is a major world language and is spoken as a first language in many countries and as an additional language in many more.

● On the map, name and label as many countries as you can where English is spoken as a first language (for example, label Australia L¹) and as an additional language (for example, India L²).

Here are some to start you off:

Sri Lanka	Pakistan
Trinidad	Malta
Jamaica	South Africa
Singapore	Kenya

World languages

What do you think are the languages which are most widely spoken around the world?

● Look at this list and write the languages on the map with the name of the country where they are spoken. Put them in order 1–10 against the languages you think are the most widely spoken.

Arabic

Hindi

Bengali

Japanese

Chinese

Portuguese

English

Russian

German

Spanish

To the helper:

● You may have no idea how many people speak each language! Try and think how big the populations of the countries are where these languages are spoken.
● Your child will be given the correct answers in school – don't forget to ask for them!

This activity is intended to arouse interest in world languages and language diversity. In school we will be looking more closely at language diversity as part of our schemes of work on language study and standard English.

_____and

child

_____

helper(s)

_____

did this activity together

_____and

child

_____

helper(s)

_____

did this activity together

Multilingual Britain

English is spoken just about everywhere in Britain and Ireland but not always as a first language. There are many other languages in Britain and some of them have been here much longer than English!

● Look at the map, can you place any of these languages in regions, towns or cities where they are spoken by a community? Mark the regions with different colours and label them.

● Use the list of places and match them up with languages, label them on your map.

Arabic
Bengali (India and Bangladesh)
Chinese
Cornish
Gaelic
Greek
Gujerati (India)
Hindi (India)
Punjabi (India and Pakistan)
Spanish
Turkish
Ukranian
Urdu (Pakistan)
Welsh
Yiddish (Jewish)
Yoruba (Nigeria)

Glasgow
Bradford
Halifax
Birmingham
Leicester
Soho
Stamford Hill
Hackney
Stoke Newington
Haringey
Paddington
Tower Hamlets
Kensington
Southall
Wembley
Wales
Cornwall
Scottish highlands

Chinese ideas

In English, letters represent sounds but in some writing systems such as Chinese, a single symbol represents an idea. Here are some examples:

dog	sheep	human	father	fruit	arrow	rice
犬	羊	人	父	実	矢	米

tree	woods	forest	school	book	sister	home
禾	林	森	校	本	妹	家

king	woman	cold	moon	bright	morning	man
王	女	寒	月	明	朝	男

day	fire	water	ice	mountain	river	good
日	火	水	氷	山	川	良

clothes	stone	right	old	mouth
衣	石	右	古	口

These signs are called ideographs.

● Write a message or a short story using these Chinese symbols or make some up of your own.

To the helper:

● Discuss the similarities and differences of some of the symbols and their meanings.

● Do you know anyone who can write Chinese and who could explain these symbols to you? Or is your local Chinese restaurant menu in dual language?

Comparing an ideographic writing system with our own alphabetic one helps children understand the nature of the symbols of written language. In school we will be looking at a variety of writing systems from around the world.

_____and

child

_____

helper(s)

_____

did this activity together

From Russia

In Russia the alphabet is written in what is known as the cyrillic script. It looks like this:

А	Б	В	Г	Д	Е	Ё	Ж	З	И	Й
a	b	v	g	d	ye	yo	zh	z	i	y

К	Л	М	Н	О	П	Р	С	Т	У	Ф
k	l	m	n	o	p	r	s	t	i	f

Х	Ц	Ч	Ш	Щ	Ъ	Ы	Ь	Э	Ю	Я
kh	ts	ch	sh	shch	'	y	'	e	yu	ya

● Translate these English words in to Russian.

Pupil _____

School _____

Shop _____

Football _____

Spelling mistake identity parade

When we make spelling mistakes they are nearly always one of the following types:

an omission: when we leave out a letter for example, litle (for little);

an addition: when we add a letter for example, missunderstand (for misunderstand);

a substitution: when we put a letter in place of another for example, independance (for independence);

an inversion: when we have all the letters correct but we swap some around for example, simpel (for simple).

● In the opening passage from Kenneth Graham's **Wind in the Willows** we have added eight spelling mistakes. Try and identify which type they are.

● Write out the type headings and put the spelling mistakes next to them.

● Don't forget to add the correct spellings of the words too.

The Mole has been working very hard all the morning, spring-cleaning his littel home. First with brooms, then with dussters; then on ladders and steps and chairs, with a brush and a pail of whitewash; til he had dust in his throat and eyes, and splashes of whitewash all over his black fur, and an acheing back and weary arms. Spring was moving in the air above and in the earth below and aruond him, penatrating even his dark and lowley litle house with its spirit of divine discontent and longing.

To the helper:

● Put a circle around the words that don't appear to be spelled correctly. Talk about what type of spelling mistake it is.
● Write out your own attempt and compare it.
● Use a dictionary to check them if you have one.

By helping children identify the types of spelling errors that are common, this activity will help improve their ability to edit and proof-read written language.

_____and

child

_____

helper(s)

_____

did this activity together

_____and

child

_____

helper(s)

_____

did this activity together

Car mechanic

What does an ignition system do?
Where would you find a bumper?
What does ABS mean?

● Become a car mechanic! Find out what the following technical terms mean and write down a description of what function they serve:

fuel pump	battery
radiator	carburettor
spark plug	bonnet
clutch	choke

Do you know any others?

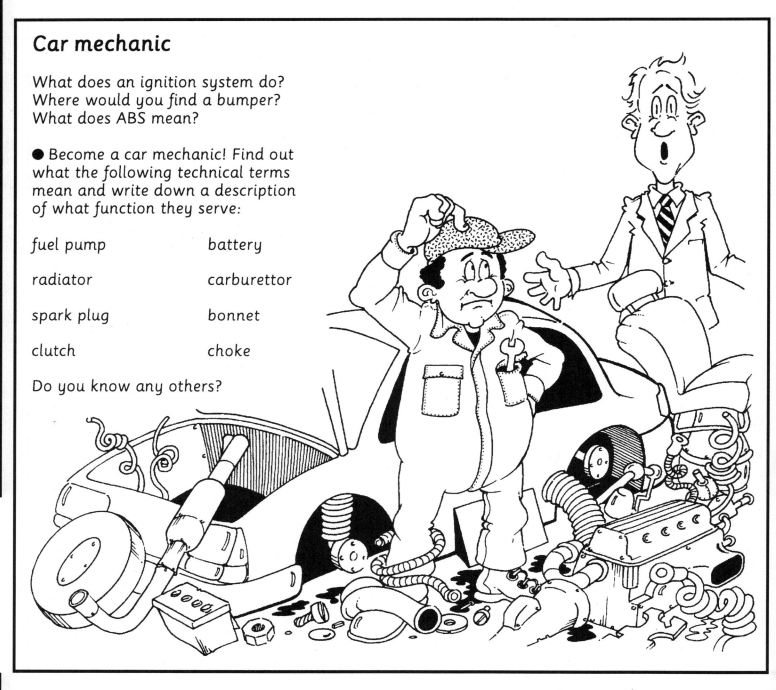

Green fingers

If you have a garden, balcony or window-box find out the names of the plants, trees or shrubs that grow in it. Do you have a local park or municipal garden where there is a shrubbery or rose garden?

Plants, trees and shrubs have Latin names (so that everyone all over the world can call them by the same name) and they have 'common' or 'popular' names (which are the names they are commonly known by in particular countries).

● Match up the Latin names of these well known trees and shrubs with their common names:

Jasmine	Lavender	Virgin's Bower
Ivy		Ilex
Clematis	Honeysuckle	Jasminum
Hedera		Holly
Lavandula	Golden Rain	Polygonum
Lonicera		Privet
Russian Vine	Laburnum	Ligustrum

To the helper:

● You don't need green fingers for this activity! Talk together and sort some of the matches by the similarity of their names.

● For others, you could use a dictionary or any gardening books or magazines you may have.

This activity focuses on the use of proper nouns and familiarises children with the convention of Latin naming and popular naming. This system is in use in many areas such as biology, horticulture and medicine.

_____and

child

_____

helper(s)

_____

did this activity together

_____and

child

_____

helper(s)

_____

did this activity together

World-wide proverbs

Here are some proverbs from around the world.
Learn them, you never know when they will come in handy!

English: Least said, soonest mended

Latin: Praemonitus, praemunitus
              'Forewarned is forearmed'

Chinese: ai wu ji wu
              'If you love a house, you love its crows'
              (which is a bit like the English: 'Love me, love my dog')

Somali: Beeni marka hore waa malab, marka dambe na waa malmal
              'Lies are honey at first, later they are myrrh'

Swahili: Mama yangu ni mwalimu wangu wa Kwanza
              'My mother was my first teacher'

Welsh: Cenedl heb iaith, cenedl heb galon
              'A nation without a language is a nation without a heart'

● Write a story about one of these proverbs,
using it in the narrative or the dialogue.

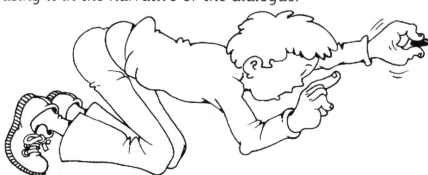

Name gamer! Anagram me!

This is (almost) an anagram. That means a word or words that can be re-arranged to make a new word or words. Here are some that work with all the letters:

astronomers = moon starers

Margaret Thatcher = Meg, the arch tarter

● Try it with your own name!

● Draw a picture to go with your anagram.

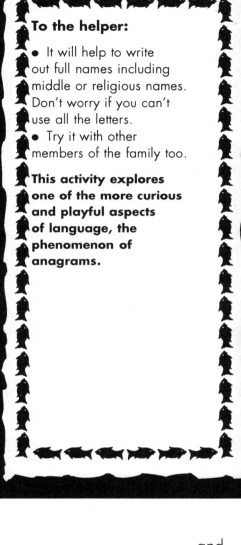

To the helper:

● It will help to write out full names including middle or religious names. Don't worry if you can't use all the letters.
● Try it with other members of the family too.

This activity explores one of the more curious and playful aspects of language, the phenomenon of anagrams.

_____and

child

_____

helper(s)

_____

did this activity together

Management

Most teachers send the shared writing task as a photocopied sheet included in the children's **Reading Folder** or in their IMPACT **Maths folder**. Remind the children that they may use the back of the IMPACT sheet to write on. Before the activity is sent home, it is crucial that the teacher prepares the children for the task. This may involve reading a story, going over some ideas or having a group or class discussion. Some ideas are provided here in the Teachers' Notes for each activity. The importance of this preparation cannot be overstressed.

Many of the tasks done at home lend themselves naturally to a display or enable the teacher to make a class-book. A shared writing display board in the entrance hall of the school gives parents an important sense that their work at home is appreciated and valued.

The shared writing activity sheets can be stuck into an exercise book kept specifically for this purpose. Any follow-up work that the children do in school can also be put into this book. As the books go back and forth with the activity sheets this enables parents to see how the work at home has linked to work in class.

Non-IMPACTers

We know that parental support is a key factor in children's education and children who cannot find anyone with whom to share the writing task may be losing out. Try these strategies:
• Encourage, cajole and reward the children who bring back their shared writing. If a child – and parent/carer – does the task haphazardly, praise the child whenever the task is completed, rather than criticise if it is not.
• If possible, invite a couple of parents in to share the activities with the children. This involves parents in the life of the school as well as making sure that some children don't lose out.
• Some schools set up 'writing partners' between children in two different classes pairing a child from Y6 with a child in Y1 for shared writing activities, perhaps weekly or fortnightly.

None of these strategies is perfect, but many parents will help when they can and with encouragement, will join in over the longer term.

Useful information and addresses

The IMPACT shared maths scheme is running successfully in thousands of schools in the UK and abroad. The shared writing works in the same way, and obviously complements the maths very well. Both fit in with the shared reading initiatives (PACT or CAPER) which many schools also run. The OFSTED Inspection Schedules require and take account of schools working with parents as well as the quality of teaching and learning. IMPACT receives positive mentions in inspectors' reports.

Further information about the IMPACT Project and IMPACT inservice training for schools or parents' groups can be obtained from: The IMPACT Project, School of Teaching Studies, University of North London, 166–220 Holloway Road, London N7 8DB.

The Shared Maths Homework books can be obtained from Scholastic Ltd, Westfield Road, Southam, Warwickshire CV33 0JH

For IMPACT Diaries contact: IMPACT Supplies, PO Box 126, Witney, Oxfordshire OX8 5YL. Tel: 01993 774408.

Curricula links

The activities in this book support the following requirements for writing in the UK national curricula for English.

National Curriculum: English, KS2 Writing
1. Range – a, b, c
2. Key Skills – a, b, c, d
3. Standard English and Language Study – a, b, c

Scottish 5-14 Guidelines: English Language	
Strand	**Level**
Spelling	C/D/E
Punctuation and structure	C/D/E
Knowledge about language	C/D/E

Northern Ireland Curriculum: English
Within meaningful contexts, pupils should be taught:
• grammatical and orthographic conventions;
• to develop use of the different conventions of writing (layout, sequencing and structure);
• the technical terms needed to describe the features of the grammar or the form of their writing.